MARATHON RUNNER'S

HANDBOOK

Bruce Fordyce
WITH MARIËLLE RENSSEN

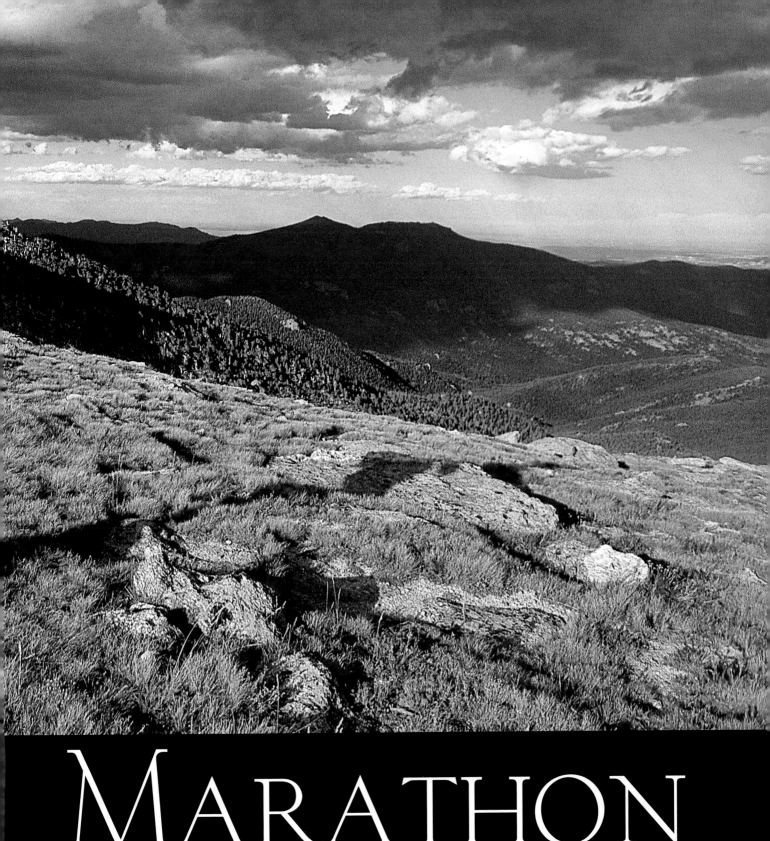

MARATHON RUNNER'S

HANDBOOK

This edition published in 2003
First published in 2002 by New Holland Publishers Ltd
London • Cape Town • Sydney • Auckland

86 Edgware Road
London W2 2EA
United Kingdom

14 Aquatic Drive
Frenchs Forest, NSW 2086
Australia

80 McKenzie Street
Cape Town 8001
South Africa

218 Lake Road
Northcote, Auckland
New Zealand

Reproduction by Hirt & Carter (Cape) Pty Ltd
Printed and bound in Malaysia by Times Offset (M) Sdn. Bhd.
10 9 8 7 6 5 4 3 2

Copyright © 2002 New Holland Publishers (UK) Ltd
Copyright © 2002 in text: Bruce Fordyce and Mariëlle Renssen
Copyright © 2002 in illustrations: New Holland Publishers (UK) Ltd
Copyright © 2002 in photographs: as credited on p160

ISBN 1 85974 723 X (hardcover)
ISBN 1 85974 724 8 (softcover)

MANAGING EDITORS	Claudia dos Santos
	Mari Roberts
MANAGING ART EDITOR	Peter Bosman
CONSULTANT EDITOR	Mariëlle Renssen
DESIGNER	Claire van Rhyn
ILLUSTRATIONS	Anton Krügel
PICTURE RESEARCHER	Zuné Roberts
INDEXER / PROOFREADER	Ingrid Corbett
PRODUCTION MANAGER	Myrna Collins
CONSULTANTS	Tim Noakes (SA), Bruce Tulloh (UK)

CONTENTS

CHAPTER SEVEN   **100** Injuries

SECTION TWO   THE MARATHON AND BEYOND

CHAPTER EIGHT   **122** From half to ultramarathon

CHAPTER NINE   **136** Memorable distance runners

CHAPTER TEN   **146** Great world marathons

INTRODUCTION

EARLY HUNTER-GATHERERS HAD TO RUN MERELY TO SURVIVE. RUNNING, THEREFORE, HAS BEEN PART OF THE HUMAN EXPERIENCE SINCE THOSE EARLY TIMES.

RUNNERS OF ANCIENT HISTORY

For the major part of humankind's presence on Earth, early humans existed by hunting and gathering food, and in the process of stalking wild animals for sustenance, early hunter-gatherers used to have to run to ensure their very survival. It is only in the last few centuries that animal husbandry, and more recently, food technology have come into being.

As far back as four million years ago, early hominids, the australopithecines, living in Africa's Rift Valley ran to catch their prey, although by studying modern hunter-gatherers (the Khoisan of Southern Africa, the Inuit of Alaska, Canada and Greenland, and the Aborigines of Australia) we understand now that hunter-gatherers spent the bulk of their mobile time walking rather than running. Nevertheless, running must have been an important part of their existence since they moved in small bands according to the changing seasons, following the herds of game and seeking the plant foods upon which they relied. They would have been naturally very fit and capable of running well when they had to. The concept of competitive running, however, would have been strange to them as they preferred to tire out their prey, pursuing the quarry stealthily and relentlessly for several days if necessary.

Structured distance racing first appeared with the Ancient Greek Olympic Games, which date back to 472BC. This event started out as a festival held every fourth year to honour Zeus, the supreme god of the heavens, in his sanctuary, ancient Olympia. Here, games and sacrifices took place over five days of festivities. While the Ancient Greeks ran distance races, none raced the length of today's marathon (42.2km; 26.2 miles). The first official marathon of this distance was raced at the 1896 Olympic Games in Athens, when a modern revival of the ancient Games took place for the first time; however, the distance was only standardized in 1908, at the Olympic Games held in London. A common belief held over the years as to how the term 'marathon' originated was that in 490BC an Athenian soldier named Pheidippides (also Philippides) ran from the Greek battlefield of Marathon to Athens with news of victory over the Persians, before dropping dead from the effort. However, only the famous Greek historian Herodotus (known as the Father of History) recorded this feat — and he wrote his history some 50 years after the battle took place. He did, however, speak to veterans of the famous battle and he was told that Pheidippides was a *hemerodromai*, or 'trained runner', and that he was sent from Athens to Sparta, a distance of over 200km (125 miles), to get help. This he had achieved in less than 48 hours.

Plutarch (AD46–120), a Greek biographer and philosopher, wrote of a soldier who, possibly wounded, brought news of the victory with the words: 'Hail, we are victorious!' and then died.

A similar story is recorded by Lucian, a second-century writer, though he identifies the soldier as Philippides. There were undoubtedly trained messengers who ran very long distances, but it is certain there was no distance remotely resembling a marathon at the Ancient Greek Olympic Games.

Among the modern runners of today, some vestige of what drove the early hunter-gatherers must remain within them, since most runners are happiest when running permits them to get back in touch with Nature. Certainly, some of my most memorable runs have not been on the streets of New York or London — or even while running a famous long-distance race — but, rather, jogging across the Southern African bushveld (sometimes in the warm rain) or in the mountains, or through a leafy forest.

TOP *These medals (gold, silver and bronze) were awarded to winning athletes in the first revival, in 1896, of the Ancient Greek Olympic Games.*

LEFT *A 19th-century painting by Thomas Tyrwhitt Balcome of a spear-carrying Aborigine; early hunter-gatherers often had to run in pursuit of prey.*

RIGHT *This amphora depicting early racing athletes of Ancient Greece dates back to the sixth century BC; the winner received the painted vessel as a prize.*

A GENETIC PHENOMENON

A great deal of research must still be done on this subject, but increasingly it is being acknowledged by experts that the ability to run certain distances appears to be better suited to specific races and cultures. This phenomenon is sometimes driven by a culturally stimulated sense of national pride; that is, certain nations have grown to believe in themselves as being particularly good at certain distance events and they are driven through patriotic zeal to continue to excel at these events. For instance, the 400m hurdles has been dominated at the highest level by US runners. They continue to excel at this distance and American colleges churn out brilliant, one-lap athletes. Hurdlers from the USA such as Ed Moses and world record holder Kevin Young underline this hypothesis.

There seems to be some truth, on the other hand, that the make-up of people of a certain race suits particular distances. A runner's best chance of winning a 100m sprint at the quadrennial Olympic Games appears to be the heritage of ancestors captured as slaves from West Africa. Unequivocally, sprinting has been dominated in the last few decades by West African athletes and though they may not be receiving the medals, their US, Canadian and British cousins certainly are benefiting: Maurice Green, Gail Devers, Florence Griffiths-Joyner, Donovan Bailey and Linford Christie can all ultimately trace their roots to West Africa, even though the medals they've won have gone to the USA, Canada and the UK.

Of course, there are exceptions, and in 1980 it was Scotsman Alan Wells who won the Olympic Games Men's 100m event. In the 1984 and 1988 Olympic Games marathons, the first place position went to Carlos Lopes of Portugal and Gelindo Bordin of Italy respectively. Try hard as they might, none of these three great runners would be able to find any trace of African ancestry in their genes!

The question of 'choosing your parents carefully' is used to describe the undeniable fact that genetic factors do play a major part in the ability to run faster and over long distances. The ideal runner's build is 'skinny', with strong legs, good cardiovascular function and lots of slow-twitch muscle fibre (see p23). This does not mean, however, that those who 'chose' their parents incorrectly cannot enjoy the sport. There are many men and women of larger build who run marathons and who enjoy all facets of distance running, so prospective runners should not shy away from the sport for reasons of not embodying the ideal runner's profile.

In the field of long-distance running, African athletes are now so dominant worldwide that in many countries, distance running

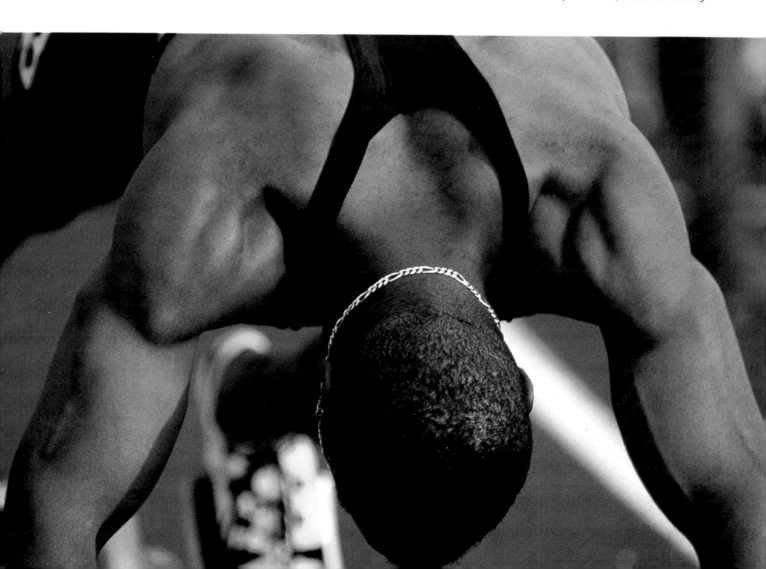

events have created a special interest for the first local runner home, offering prizes to the one who achieves this. These African distance runners are the opposite of the West African sprinters; they are the graceful, thin-boned East Africans and, to a lesser extent, Southern Africans. We have only to look at a famous race, such as the Boston Marathon (USA), over the last decade to observe the sheer dominance of the East Africans. On the one hand, they have learnt to pride themselves on their endurance running ability and to embrace it as an escape route from a life often characterized by abject poverty. On the other, there seems to be proof that these runners descended from peoples who have lived for millions of years on the edge of the Rift Valley have a distinct genetic advantage when it comes to running distances at speed. All over the world, Kenyan, Ethiopian, Ugandan and Southern African distance runners — both male and female — are highly respected, and feared as opponents. When the great American distance runner Marti Liquori was soundly beaten by Ethiopian Miruts Yifter at the 1977 World Cup in both the 5000m and 10,000m events, he was asked if he had heard of Yifter before. 'No', he replied, 'but I *have* heard of Ethiopia.'

Studies carried out by the Sports Science Institute based in Cape Town, South Africa, have shown that the muscles of black distance runners can undergo more cycles of contraction and relaxation before hitting intense fatigue than those of white runners — proving that the black athletes are more resistant to long-distance muscle fatigue.

Perhaps the most impressive example of genetic dominance comes from the modern Olympic Games. In every Olympics year in which they've competed (since 1968), Kenyan males have never lost the Men's 3000m Steeplechase. Usually they take two of the three medals on offer, sometimes all three.

There may be signs emerging now that when it comes to the ultra long-distance events of 80km (50 miles) or longer, a strain of northern Caucasians are dominant. Certainly, Russian, Scottish, Finnish and other northern European runners and their descendants have dominated ultra-running up to now.

LEFT AND RIGHT *The phenomenon of how North and East Africa has produced so many superb middle- and long-distance runners is still not fully explained. It is clear that black runners from North America, despite abundant financial backing and scholarships, have not excelled on the same scale in track and field. In East Africa, particularly, many famous runners (at right is onetime New York Marathon winner, Kenyan Joseph Chebet) can trace their heritage back to the Cushitic and Nilotic tribes, pastoralists from the Great Rift Valley. It is believed they may have evolved a genetic advantage, influenced by factors such as a protein-rich diet based on cow's milk and unrefined cereals and grains, and a pastoral lifestyle following herds across high, hilly country.*

GETTING 'HOOKED' ON RUNNING

All this scientific reasoning detracts from the simple joy and appeal that can be gained from distance running. Just because a runner's name does not begin with Kip [Keino], or the runner has never seen Addis Ababa, does not mean that he or she cannot enjoy the sport. Olympic glory may be out of the question, but the challenge and attendant health benefits are available to everyone. Anyone who has recently become 'addicted' to distance running will attest to the power it has to get people firmly 'hooked'. It is quite extraordinary, since many beginners describe distance running as: 'Boring at the best of times, boring and painful at the worst.' Somehow, though, it has 'hooked' millions of runners all over the world.

Runners give many reasons for why they started out to run: to lose a little extra weight; to become fit; to nurture the streak of competitiveness they have within; to gain some 'time out' from their daily pressures; or simply to get out into Nature. Also, running is an easy sport to begin as it doesn't require expensive equipment (other than the initial investment of a pair of good running shoes), venues don't have to be booked ahead of time, and it can be fitted into your personal schedule in a way that suits only you — either in the early mornings before work or before daily chores, at lunchtime, or in the evenings after work.

In the end, running gives everyone a chance to be a winner. By finishing a 10km (6-mile) race, be it in 30, 40, 50 or over 60 minutes, you conquer your most important foe: yourself. Runners win by actually completing that marathon, even though they may be several hours behind the actual winner. It doesn't stop them from feeling the same sense of euphoria, or runner's 'high', after prolonged exercise as the more elite runners, and it is a very powerful 'hook', particularly so for those who began running unfit and out of shape. The medals, badges and T-shirts that are given out at races are also very compelling. It is amazing what self-pride and sense of achievement is generated just by you having earned the right to your medal or to wear the T-shirt that commemorates the race.

Staying 'Hooked'

Runners are a little like drug addicts. Once they're under its spell, they yearn for their daily (or regular) 'hit' of natural morphine — which occurs in the human body in the form of endorphins, chemicals released by the brain and recognized as a morphine-like substance. When runners cannot achieve this, they become irritable and impatient. Humans are creatures of habit; once running has become a way of life, it forms part of their daily routine and becomes as important as eating breakfast for that boost to start the day.

The health benefits of running also help to hook runners. After having made the decision to give running a try, improved health becomes obvious within a few weeks of regular outings. Over time these outings lead to reduced weight, fat replaced by lean tissue, cardiovascular improvement and a stronger heart, and a generally improved lifestyle (runners tend to give up smoking, eat more healthily and drink less alcohol). This is particularly true in the case of runners who have started relatively late in life, after a long sedentary lifestyle. Those who started and found themselves unable to run a single kilometre without stopping to breathe are often amazed — and delighted — at their progress. Positive reinforcement of a runner's appearance keeps him or her hooked. The newly slimmer and leaner runner looks good and will draw compliments from friends and family. Famous American runner Frank Shorter once said: 'I run because I don't want to feel the way you look.' New converts fear going back to their old unfit state once they've learnt to enjoy their new, stronger bodies.

Finally, psychologists have long understood the value and power of 'play'. As adults we often forget to play, and so lose out on many of its benefits — both emotional and physical. It is said that when Africa's great Zulu king, Chaka, wished to punish his troops (the famous *impi*), he would order them to follow a child for a day, doing everything the child did. Even the fittest of his soldiers were exhausted by the end of the day — but they had learnt a great deal.

Running can give adults the chance to rediscover the benefits of 'playtime'. Yes, it is structured playtime, but it can be considered play — or 'time out'. It is vital to recognize that we are very often too serious and tend to get locked into excessive 'worktime', allowing ourselves no respite.

In summary the question is, actually, not why so many runners *get* hooked, but why so many have not yet *become* hooked!

TOP *Communing with Nature is an important part of running; as every city has its parks, even office-bound individuals are able to get into the outdoors.*
RIGHT *Every relatively new runner will attest to the fact that an incredible sense of achievement in attaining the personal goals they set themselves is what keeps them firmly 'hooked' on running.*

SECTION ONE

HOW TO BECOME A SERIOUS RUNNER

THERE IS NO SECRET FORMULA OR MAGIC TRICK TO RUNNING. HARD WORK IS THE KEY.
BUT HARD WORK BASED ON COMMON SENSE, A GREAT DEAL OF CAUTION — AND FUN.

PHYSIOLOGY

THE HEALTH BENEFITS OF RUNNING ARE NUMEROUS, VERY WELL DOCUMENTED, AND IF CONSCIOUSLY TAKEN ON CAN LEAD TO A LIFETIME OF WELLBEING.

IMPROVE YOUR HEALTH

Scientific studies have shown that the human body is designed to be tested physically, and that it rewards those who do so — as long as runners are sensible about their activity and take care to treat their body well.

The results of a study on fit and active males undertaken by an aerobics research institute, the Cooper Institute, based in Dallas (USA), concluded that runners and healthy, exercising individuals generally lived between six and 12 years longer than unfit, sedentary people.

Being 'sensible' means going for a regular medical check-up — particularly before embarking on a running schedule when the runner concerned is aware of known risks in his or her state of health. It also means listening to your body and recognizing when you should not be running, for example, when you are ill or injured, or you are running a temperature.

Cardiac Strengthening

There are definitely cardiac benefits to running. Over time and with training, the heart as a muscle strengthens. The power of each heartbeat thus increases, leading to a decreased heart rate, and as a result the heart becomes more efficient (when exercising, a fit heart pumps 50 per cent more blood than an unfit one). Suffice it to say that a stronger heart is an eminently healthier one, and it has been widely proven that fitness reduces the risk of coronary heart failure (heart attack).

An improved cardiovascular system ensures that blood is pumped to the fine capillaries in the furthest extremities of the body (see illustration on p18). These tiny capillaries also increase in the working muscles, bringing an essential blood supply to all areas of the human frame. At the same time, regular physical exercise such as running maintains a healthy inner lining to the body's blood vessels, making artery blockages a less likely occurrence.

Superior Lung Capacity

In terms of a runner's lung capacity, any doctor will report that the functioning of runners' lungs is vastly superior to those of sedentary people. Their lungs are stronger, more expansive and expel inhaled smoke, gas and foreign matter more efficiently than their less fit counterparts.

After the death, at age 69, of the great American marathon runner, Clarence de Mar, who won the Boston Marathon an incredible seven times in the early decades of the 1900s, an autopsy was performed on his body (he died of bowel cancer but the autopsy set out to substantiate that he had suffered from heart problems). His cardiovascular system was found to be in a condition similar to that of a young man in his twenties — years of running had added tremendous health benefits to his circulatory system.

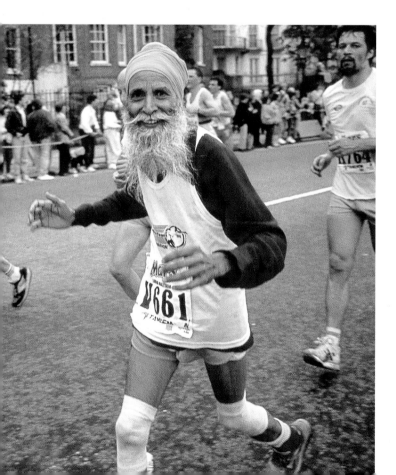

LEFT AND RIGHT *Running is definitely not limited to the young and virile. On the contrary, many runners start the sport relatively late in life and in most cases this becomes a healthy commitment which leads to extraordinary wellbeing in one's later years in life.*

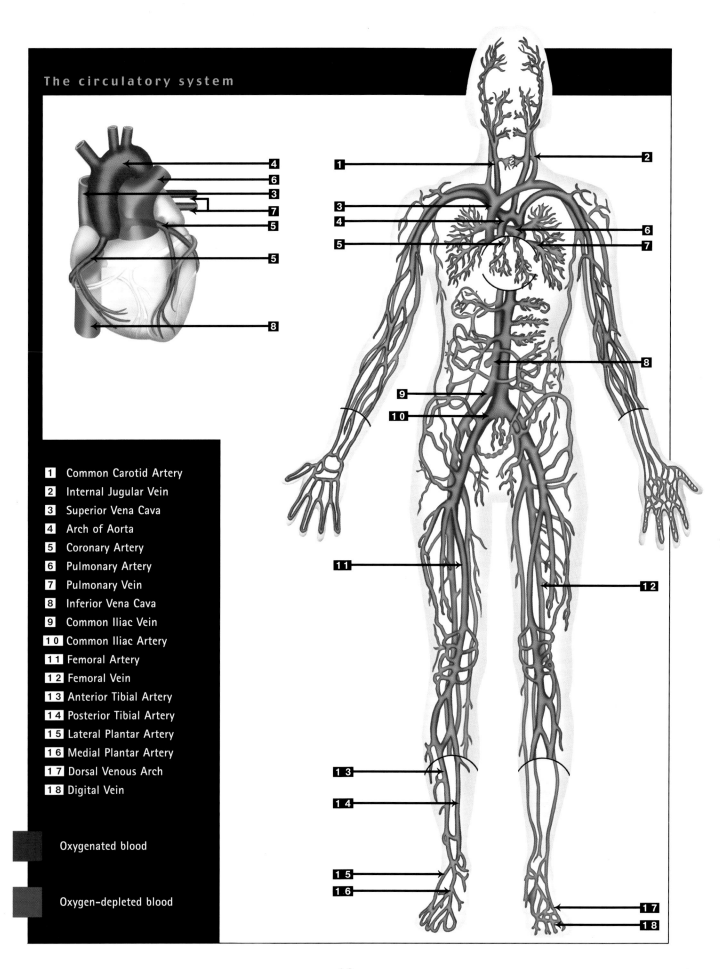

1 Common Carotid Artery
2 Internal Jugular Vein
3 Superior Vena Cava
4 Arch of Aorta
5 Coronary Artery
6 Pulmonary Artery
7 Pulmonary Vein
8 Inferior Vena Cava
9 Common Iliac Vein
10 Common Iliac Artery
11 Femoral Artery
12 Femoral Vein
13 Anterior Tibial Artery
14 Posterior Tibial Artery
15 Lateral Plantar Artery
16 Medial Plantar Artery
17 Dorsal Venous Arch
18 Digital Vein

Oxygenated blood

Oxygen-depleted blood

Lowering Cholesterol Levels

All exercise, particularly running, has been proved beneficial to the consistency of the blood, particularly in terms of cholesterol. This is a waxy insoluble substance that is produced in the liver and also absorbed from foods that come from animal sources. It is carried through the blood by lipoproteins. HDLs (high-density lipoproteins) contain a small amount of cholesterol and act by carrying excess cholesterol from the tissues to the liver, while LDLs (low-density lipoproteins) carry the highest volume of cholesterol and are responsible for depositing it on the body's artery walls. Because of the different levels of cholesterol carried, HDLs are termed "good" and LDLs "bad" cholesterol. Regular exercise improves the ratio of HDL to LDL, where HDLs act as a "pipe cleaner," scouring away the LDL, which is the cause of deposit build-up, or plaque, on the artery walls of the coronary and other arteries. Sometimes the plaque blocks blood circulation to the heart or brain, cutting off the supply of oxygen to the organs, and part of the tissue dies. This is what occurs during a heart attack or stroke. If a person reduces a high cholesterol level by 25 per cent, he or she will decrease the risk of a heart attack by as much as 50 per cent.

With time and training effort, it is inevitable that an exercising person's body weight will decrease. More lean muscle tissue develops and the runner's metabolism increases as a result of the increase in working muscle mass.

RIGHT *The heart, lungs and blood vessels work together to ensure a constant circulation of blood through the body. A heart that has been strengthened through sustained exercise such as running pumps blood more strongly. This increased circulation also results in more efficient penetration of the often neglected extremities, providing better nourishment of the muscles and cells.*

Keeping the Joints "Oiled"

One of the criticisms aimed at runners and their health is that running stiffens the joints, speeds up the onset of arthritis, and worse still, injures the joints. This is simply not the case. Generally, joints are poorly supplied by blood mainly because of their complex reticulated structure of bone and cartilage without the presence of major blood vessels, but in runners, because of the more efficient circulatory processes improved by the exercise, the blood supply is increased to these areas so bones and joints work more efficiently. Latent injuries to joints are more often *exposed* by running rather than *caused* by it. In other words, old rugby, football and hockey injuries that would not normally be noticed by a sedentary 40-year-old suddenly flare up once that person decides to take up running years after having given up other physical pursuits. Rather, running is the "messenger" — which brings the bad news of the dormant damage wreaked by the earlier rough contact sports.

Although it is sometimes said that too much running can deplete the body's bone structure of minerals such as calcium, magnesium

and potassium, this is actually a dietary problem. It has been conclusively proven that moderate, sensible running actually increases the supply of calcium and other minerals to the bone. Most of the body's calcium is stored in the bones, and high-impact exercise, by placing additional stress on the femur, tibia and fibula bones of the legs, sets in motion a strengthening process which builds up the bone density. The increase in bone calcification makes them become stronger and more resilient.

A Healthier Lifestyle

Often without specifically setting out to do so, runners tend to become more health-conscious through a keenness to further their fitness, which then leads to their need to explore other options of

NOTHING REPLACES TIME AS A BUILDER OF GREAT DISTANCE RUNNERS. YOU NEED TO RUN FOR A LONG TIME TO BUILD UP ENDURANCE AND STRENGTH — AND STEADY PROGRESS ONLY COMES WITH TIME.

doing so. A healthier lifestyle is a natural progression to cutting down on excessive fats in their diet, and avoiding junk food binges and unhealthy takeout meals. Runners may decide to give up smoking (because it is affecting their lung capacity) and although they will often still drink alcohol, they will tend to drink more selectively, especially before a run. What is likely is that they end up drinking far less than others.

Running Stimulates the Brain

Many runners report that they need their running time to be alone with their thoughts. Many others de-stress by running, while there are those who believe that running stimulates creativity in the mind. This is not an imagined phenomenon — it is quite true that the increased blood supply to the brain through activity stimulates the thinking and creative parts of the brain. Many runners plan work strategies, write articles, prepare speeches and even create poetry in their heads while pounding the pavement. Certainly, for myself, many a difficult creative task such as a speech or essay has been composed by my "running" brain.

One of the most surprising health benefits of running is its ability to improve the psychological make-up of a person. To make that decision to start running, you have to believe that you can do it because it does take self-discipline, effort and commitment, especially if you don't have the convenience of a running partner to nudge you on or you can't afford a personal coach. The motivation has to come entirely from yourself.

But as soon as you start seeing the results, you will find that it becomes a personal challenge to improve in what may start out to be small steps. However, as you achieve each small challenge this leads to the next, slightly bigger, goal. And an enormous sense of pride is gained by achieving that goal.

There is no doubt that runners have a higher self-esteem than those people who don't exercise at all; as their bodies become more toned and fit, runners get to like the way they look, and this increased self-respect leads to greater confidence. Runners feel a sense of having control over their destiny and of being a player in life rather than a spectator.

There is much published literature supporting the fact that many runners have found the confidence they've gained through running manifesting itself in other areas of their lives. Often in becoming more extrovert, they find themselves making new friends and even, sometimes, being promoted.

Demystifying muscle terminology	
Muscle	Complex body tissue that contracts and relaxes to produce motion
Tendon	Tough fibrous connective tissue that attaches muscle to bone
Ligament	Tough band of tissue that connects the two parts of a bone joint; also holds organs in place

THE PHYSIOLOGY OF RUNNING

The most essential component of running is the contraction produced by skeletal muscle, which itself relies on a supply of energy, created by a chemical reaction in the body, to properly function.

STRUCTURE AND WORKING OF MUSCLES

Each muscle in the body consists of myriad muscle cells, or fibers. These fibers are a complex, integrated structure made up of many elements within elements. The muscle cells receive blood and nerve signals from tiny capillaries and nerves in the connective tissue that exists around each cell. Within each muscle fiber are large numbers of parallel-lying myofibrils, which themselves contain a host of what are called sarcomeres. Within those elongated parallel sarcomeres are the myofilaments — composed of a thick filament (myosin) and a thin one (actin). The interplay between these two elements produces muscle contraction.

Just as essential to the working of the muscle are the mitochondria, which are situated around the myofibrils. These are responsible for supplying the muscle with energy. Enzymes in the mitochondria harness oxygen to transform energy from the foods we take in into ATP (adenosine triphosphate) molecules (see p25). In its metabolized form of ADP and phosphate, the body makes use of energy for all its growth, development and repair processes.

Energy Sources for Working Muscles
Carbohydrates and fats The muscles make use of two sources of energy to function well. Carbohydrates stored in the liver and muscle cells as glycogen are converted to glucose and either released into the bloodstream or, in the case of the glycogen stored in the muscles, taken up immedi-

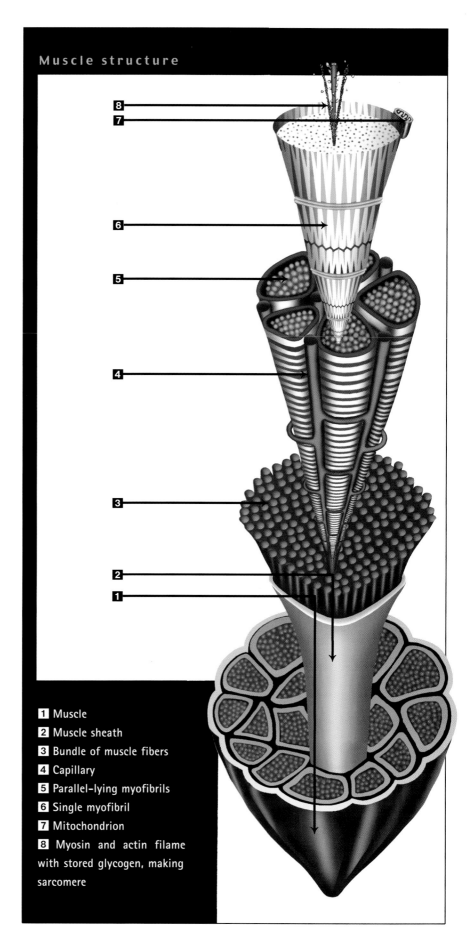

Muscle structure

1 **Muscle**
2 **Muscle sheath**
3 **Bundle of muscle fibers**
4 **Capillary**
5 **Parallel-lying myofibrils**
6 **Single myofibril**
7 **Mitochondrion**
8 **Myosin and actin filame with stored glycogen, making sarcomere**

ately for contraction. Secondly, fat stored in the muscle cells in the form of triglyceride molecules is broken down to fatty acids and glycerol. An enzyme called lipase is the catalyst for the fat breakdown process. The fatty acids (known now as "free" fatty acids) are released into the bloodstream to be transported to the mitochondria of the muscle cells. The glycerol molecules that are freed up in the chemical reaction travel to the liver where they are used for glucose production.

The breakdown of triglycerides, which is a more slow-releasing form of energy, is very important for runners taking part in endurance exercise over long distances such as marathons and the ultramarathons — where duration rather than intensity is the focus.

Without oxygen Although most functioning of the body requires oxygen, in certain situations muscle contraction can take place without it within fluid known as sarcoplasm, which surrounds the mitochondria and myofilaments. Enzymes contained within the sarcoplasm cause a series of chemical reactions (requiring no oxygen) which produce energy that can be used by the body for its various working processes, including muscle contraction.

Types of Muscle Fiber

There are two types of muscle cell, referred to as Type I and Type II. They are also defined as "slow-twitch" and "fast-twitch" muscles.

Type I are red due to their high proportion of myoglobin (a red protein pigment

RIGHT *Runners can improve their speed and running efficiency by training their muscles to adapt to different paces and intensities. For example, sprinting and bouts of fast running force the muscles to function anaerobically (without oxygen), so muscles need to learn to cope with this.*

containing iron and similar to haemoglobin) and they carry large numbers of mitochondria. The myoglobin ferries oxygen carried by the blood to the mitochondria; it also stores oxygen in the muscles. Type I are slow-twitch muscles, which refers to the fact that they are slower to contract and relax than their fast-twitch counterpart. *Type II* muscle fibers are white due to a low quantity of myoglobin. They also have fewer mitochondria. Type II are fast-twitch muscles.

Scientific studies have shown that the muscles of sprinters contain a high percentage of fast-twitch fibers while those of long-distance runners feature a high proportion of slow-twitch fibers. Middle-distance runners, cyclists and swimmers have more of a balance between the two fiber types.

Concentric and Eccentric Muscle Contraction

Concentric muscle contraction occurs when muscle contracts and shortens. Eccentric contraction, on the other hand, is when the muscle lengthens while attempting the contraction process — and it is forced to do so when the muscle is load-bearing (that is, carrying the body's weight) and the weight of that load is more forceful than the muscle's attempt to contract.

Runners can feel this process in their quadriceps (upper thigh muscles) when they are running a downhill. The force being applied to the quadriceps is quite considerable — on striking the ground, the feet sometimes take three times the body weight. It is obvious, therefore, why downhill running can lead to muscle injury and also why runners often experience delayed muscle soreness after tackling a course that incorporates such downhills.

ENERGY BREAKDOWN OF FOOD

The stomach contains digestive enzymes which act on the carbohydrates and proteins we take in. The enzymes break down the carbohydrates into glucose, galactose (less soluble and less sweet

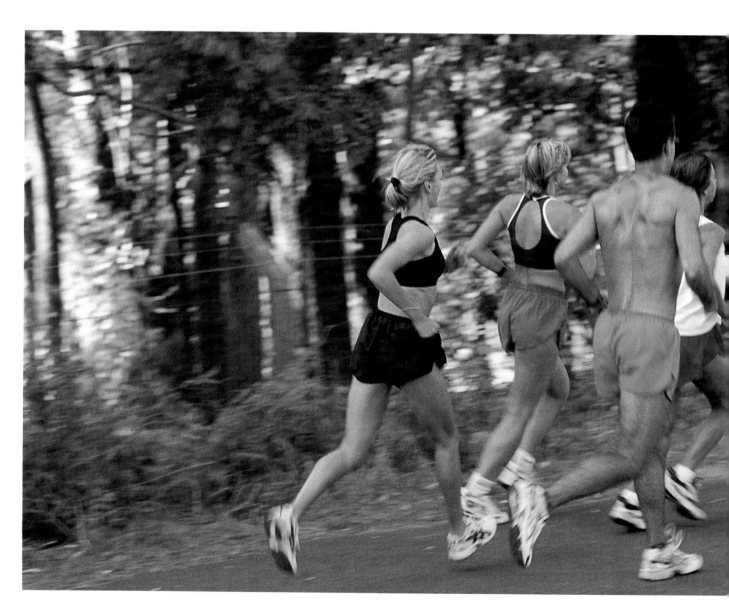

than glucose), maltose (fermentable sugars from starch) and fructose (fruit and honey), and the proteins into amino acids.

The carbohydrate components are then transported to the liver, which converts them to glucose after which they are stored as glycogen. Glucose is also transported to the muscles to be stored as muscle glycogen.

When the body and its muscles need energy, the glycogen stores are metabolized into glucose and absorbed into the bloodstream for use. From here the chemical reaction in which ATP (adenosine triphosphate) is broken down to ADP (adenosine diphosphate) for energy begins. Simply put, a group of molecules in the muscle cells known as ATP — which occurs in combination with three phosphate molecules — harnesses the glycogen energy; when high-energy bonds connecting the ATP molecule-groups are broken in a chemical reaction they re-form as ADP and phosphate, and energy is released. It is this energy that initiates contraction of the muscles.

ADP is converted back to ATP to continue the cycle. Amino acids also travel to the liver where they play a part in producing glucose and glycogen. In addition, they replace damaged proteins in muscle and other body tissue.

Fats are sent to the adipose tissue (connective tissue beneath the skin where the body stores its fat in the form of droplets) where they are stored as triglycerides.

BELOW LEFT *Easy slow running over long distances (more than one and a half hours) is excellent fat-burning exercise, good news for joggers who are looking to their running as a means of losing some weight. Because the body can only store a limited amount of glycogen in the muscles, once these stores have been depleted, the working body turns to the triglycerides — fatty acids stored in the body's fat tissues — as a source of energy. It is also a more slow-burning form of energy and is therefore good for endurance exercise.*

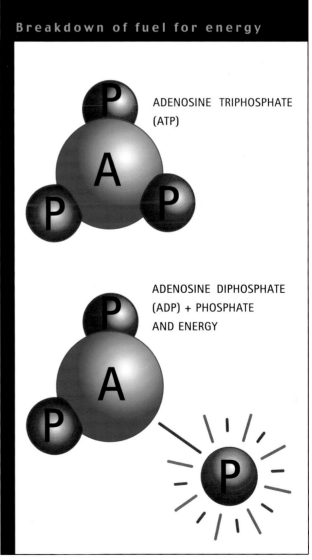

Breakdown of fuel for energy

ADENOSINE TRIPHOSPHATE (ATP)

ADENOSINE DIPHOSPHATE (ADP) + PHOSPHATE AND ENERGY

RUNNING GEAR

YOUR FOOT TYPE

Although footwear is considered to be key to injury-free running, there are, of course, exceptions. Runners such as Ethiopian Abebe Bikila and South African Zola Budd didn't believe that shoes were that important — and they were well qualified to assert this: Bikila won the Rome Olympic Marathon in 1960 running barefoot over the city's cobblestones, and Budd was famous as a teenager for her barefoot track running in the 1980s. Generally, however, protection and proper support for the feet is the best way to avoid injury.

Essentially runners fall into one of three categories and these relate to foot strike and push-off. When our feet strike the ground, they do one of three things: they either pronate, supinate or remain neutral. There is no perfect foot strike and each of these three patterns has its advantages and disadvantages. You can get an idea of your foot type by standing barefoot on firm sand (or with wet feet on a bathmat) and observing the imprint it leaves (see diagram).

PRONATORS

Pronators, of which I am one, strike the ground with the outside and back of the heel. They roll on the foot, taking off on the ball of the big toe, the ankle having tilted markedly inwards. In excessive pronators, the foot can appear to bend inwards to such an extent as to give the appearance of running alongside the shoe's inner edge. Pronation is excellent for shock absorption but can cause injury to the knees, ankles and to the muscles involved in holding the foot firmly. Injuries are common in the calf muscles: the soleus and gastrocnemius muscles. (Before I corrected my pronation tendency, I suffered many injuries to the soleus muscles.) These are connected by the Achilles tendon which also attaches them to the heel bone. Pronators are called "splat" foot runners.

SUPINATORS

Supinators have high-arched feet; they land on the outside of the foot and roll outwards, thus failing to provide any shock absorption for the foot. They have a distinct toe action in running and can

TOP *Today's high-tech shoes are carefully designed to provide flexibility and cushioned support to protect jarring of the limbs.*

RIGHT *Ninety per cent of Kenya's elite distance runners belong to the Kalenjin and Kisii tribes. Their prowess is attributed both to East Africa's high-altitude training grounds and a diet of mainly natural, unrefined foods such as corn.*

		Analyzing your foot type	
Pronator	"Splat"		
Neutral	Neutral		
Supinator	"Clunk"		

It is important to learn as early as possible what one's strengths and weaknesses are in terms of one's personal biomechanics. After one or two injuries early on in my running career, I learned that I had a severe overpronation problem, particularly in my left foot. I am therefore prone to injuries directly related to pronation and as a result, have suffered injuries to both my left and right soleus (calf) muscles — responsible for holding the feet and ankles steady. I have also suffered from a bout of plantar fasciitis (tearing of the fibrous tissue on the underside of the foot). To correct this problem, I do the bulk of my training in firm, supportive running shoes that help to correct the pronation tendency (orthotics did not work for me, so I have sought out an off-the-shelf shoe design that accommodates my foot shape). I can still get away with racing in shoes that are lightweight and offer little support; but I must ensure that I do not overdo the number of runs I undertake in this type of shoe.

DIAGRAM INDICATES RIGHT FOOT ONLY

SUPINATION   NEUTRAL   PRONATION

appear to be slightly bow-legged as opposed to the knock-kneed appearance of the pronator.

They risk injury to the muscles on the outside of the leg and also to their hips and knees. Supinators can be susceptible to iliotibial band friction syndrome (more commonly known as ITBS), referring to the tendon that extends from the hip across the outside of the knee and into the tibia, below the knee joint (see chapter on Injuries). They tend, too, to have tight Achilles tendons and will therefore be prone to Achilles-related injuries, such as tendonitis. Supinators are also known as "clunk" foot runners.

NEUTRAL RUNNERS

The feet of this category of runner display a combination of elements from the above foot type. Because of this, it is not necessary to select a shoe that has special motion control or cushioning features. Neutral runners have the least chance of injury but must again be wary of doing too much training, too often, too quickly.

BUYING YOUR SHOES

The difficult part of deciding on a running shoe is that there is a dazzling and often confusing array from which to choose today. Apart from the famous brand names like Reebok, Nike, Adidas, Puma, Asics, New Balance, Mizuno and so on, there are also several shoe designs within each brand. All are created for different purposes, different builds of runner and varying distances. It is a far cry from the 1960s when there were only one or two brands and hardly any choice. Before that runners used sand or tennis shoes and cut off the hard, rubberized toe guards to allow for movement of their toes. They also lined the shoes with soap to avoid blisters!

Many runners look to their idols in making their decisions on what shoes to wear, and shoe companies, aware of this, sponsor the leading athletes with both equipment and lucrative financial deals. Runners must recognize that for many of these leading sportsmen, their shoes are custom-built and crafted. Just because Ethiopian running star Hailie Gebrselassie wears a particular racing shoe does not necessarily mean its brand and model will propel other runners to achieve great times. What a shoe can do, if properly selected, is ensure that a runner runs in comfort, and injury-free.

Shoes have come a long way since the running boom began in the mid-1920s: they were fairly heavy and had little real cushioning and support. In the 1970s Bill Bowerman, a running coach at the University of Oregon, began experimenting in his garage with rubber and a waffle iron. In partnership with Phil Knight he formed the Nike shoe company, named after the Greek goddess of Victory. Today the company is worth billions. Other shoe companies followed suit and shoe technology exploded; so, too, did design and color. Now we have shoes in tangerine-orange and lime-green, with air- or gel-injected soles; shoes with tread patterns that would make a moon-walking astronaut proud. We have complex lacing systems and lightweight rubbers and plastics like EVA (ethylene vinyl acetate), today the most commonly used mid-sole foam due to its lightness, resilience and good cushioning qualities. We even have shoes that contain a microchip which records each run, and when downloaded onto a computer, records the distance run, calories consumed and predicted fitness increase and weight loss.

Major shoe manufacturer New Balance developed a shoe that offers comfortable fitting for the varying widths of large, medium or narrow feet. In addition to this there are sock-fitting shoes (that fit the foot as snugly and streamlined as a sock), transparent plastic shoes, cross-country and heavy terrain shoes as well as spikes for sprinters and air spikes for distance track races.

If you make a mistake by buying a pair of shoes that does not suit you, much money can be wasted. Avoid the big chain stores when buying shoes; rather go to the small expert sports and running-shoe shops. The shoes will cost more but you will save a lot of money by being given expert advice immediately and by being guided to the shoes that best suit your running biomechanics (the study of human movement) and your requirements. It would be an advantage to have some knowledge of any potential pronation/supination tendency you have before choosing a shoe.

With time you may develop a friendly relationship with your running-shoe shop-owner and will feel confident about his or her guiding you to the correct choice. At the same time, you will also become more tuned in to your own biomechanics.

ABOVE *Rapidly advancing technology and the intense competition between major shoe brands has promoted a constant refinement in the support and protection that the shoe — the most important item of equipment for the runner — can offer. Among the most famous innovations have been Asics' gel-compound midsoles and Nike's sealed, compressed-air canals.*

AT THE END OF MY FASTEST COMRADES MARATHON [5:24:07] IN 1986, I KNEW THAT MY SHOES WERE PERFECT BECAUSE I HAD NOT NOTICED THEM AT ALL DURING THE RACE.

CHOOSING YOUR SHOES

The first factor in making your selection is to establish the purpose for which the shoes will be used. Obviously there are specialist shoes for track and field and for cross-country running, but the vast majority of distance runners are exclusively road runners — and even the elite track runners end up spending the bulk of their training time on the road.

The most important shoes any runner can own are training shoes. These should have long-wearing, supportive and cushioning attributes. Many runners try to buy the lightest shoe possible, but remember, even with today's feather-light materials, lightness in a shoe generally lacks satisfactory support and cushioning. Tired, battered legs are more susceptible to injury and are less likely to be able to run longer distances. Choose a training shoe for support and cushioning long before you choose it for weight and looks.

Depending on your weight and running style, shoes will generally require replacing every nine months for the beginner runner (every four to six months for the serious marathoner). The annual shoe survey run by *Runner's World* calculates that a good pair of shoes should last for 650–800km (400–500 miles), that is, 30km per week over a 6-month period. Never throw old trainers away, however, as they are always useful as back-up shoes.

Also note that the most expensive shoe is not always the best shoe. The testing factor is whether it suits your personal biomechanics.

LEFT *The rate of wear and tear on your racing shoes and the frequency with which you will need to replace them depends very much on the type of terrain you choose to run on — and the number of long races you participate in. If you enjoy cross-country running, your shoes will take a battering much faster than running on flat easy courses.*

The secret of tying laces

It is important to find a lacing system that works well for you. The shoe should be held snug around the foot, but no part of the foot should be constricted or restricted. Too much lace-induced pressure in one spot can result in blisters or tender inflammation.

▸ Feel free to experiment and thread laces through only those eyelets that result in a comfortable fit.

▸ When you are running a race, make sure you tie a double knot in your laces.

1 Relieves pressure to top of feet

2 Is less restrictive for feet with a high instep

3 Reduces volume for narrow feet

4 Prevents heel slippage as well as black toenails

RACING SHOES

While most runners understand that they must train in suitably supportive running shoes to avoid injury, many like to wear ultra-lightweight racers for a distance race. These shoes are only worn for racing and offer the barest minimum in support and cushioning. The idea on race day, of course, is to feel — and to be — as light and strong as possible.

Lacing up a shoe that can be balanced on one finger is the final act of racing commitment. Racing shoes have a huge psychological role to play: they prepare the runner for the race effort and they help to make him or her feel that everything possible has been done to ensure a fast run. Your racing shoes do not require much wear-

ing in. A couple of training runs, a short distance race or two — and the shoes are ready for combat. These shoes are kept specifically for races and, particularly in the case of ultramarathon runners, after being worn in a good handful of events are often ready to be discarded (beginner runners will not need to replace their shoes as often). If they are worn sparingly and only in races, there is little danger of injury. However, it is important to avoid the temptation to wear them for training because prolonged usage can result in injury. Every serious runner (one who is in training for a specific race and not simply running to keep in prime health) should own at least two pairs of training shoes — even of the same model — wearing them alternately. One pair of racing shoes is sufficient.

Heel tab

Heel counter

Last

Outer sole

Midsole

Insole

Orthotic
(fitted here where necessary)

Upper

Toe box

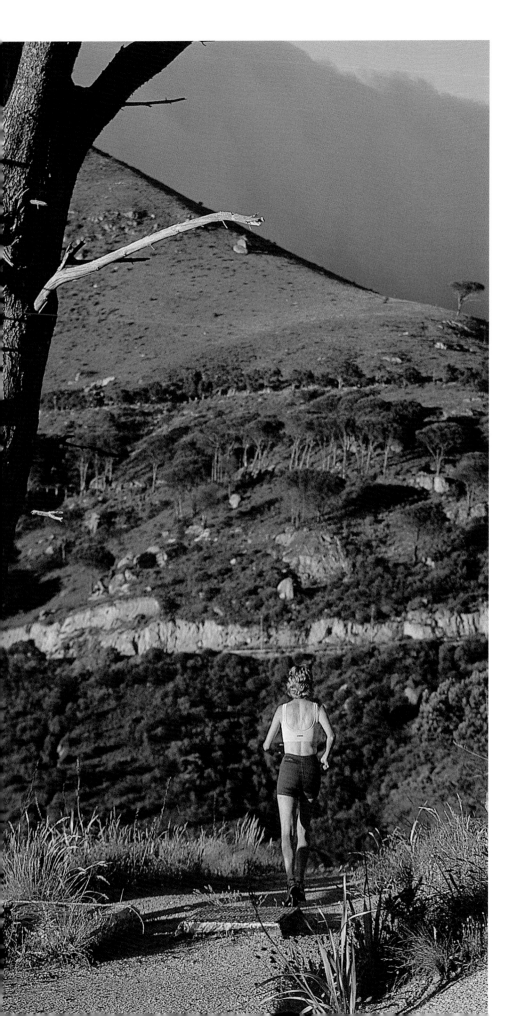

CUTTING THROUGH SHOE JARGON

Together with the latest shoe technology comes a wealth of jargon that is very confusing to a beginner runner. Below is a rundown of a shoe's main components.

Last

Although a last also refers to the wooden or metal form used as a mould for the making of a shoe, in a runner's terms it generally refers to the firm base that determines the shape of the shoe as seen from its underside.

Lasts are designed either curved (that is, there is a slight angle midway between heel and toe) or straight, with the intent to stabilize the foot.

The straight-lasted shoe has firm midsoles, and for those runners who tend to roll inwards it helps resist ankle pronation and gives good control and support to the foot. Curved lasts allow for increased foot movement rather than control for those who supinate (and thus have higher arches) and they provide more cushioning for better shock absorption.

A good shoe flexibility test is to twist the heel and toe in opposite directions to check the shoe for resistance and ascertain the measure of support it will give to the ankle. (Board-lasted shoes, i.e. a board overlies the midsole, are more supportive.)

Heel Counter

The heel counter stabilizes the foot in the shoe, holding the back of the foot firmly in place. Usually made of plastic or suede, it is vital in preventing excessive mobility of the ankle.

LEFT *Because distance running is such a high-impact sport affecting the muscles, tendons and ligaments of one's legs, knees and feet, a shoe that offers good foot control and support is extremely important for injury-free running.*

Midsole

The midsole is the central, cushioning layer of the shoe that softens the impact of running. It is often made of several rubber derivatives and helps to soften the repeated blows of a runner's strides. It also needs to support the ankle, aiding against pronation, but should have a certain degree of flexibility allowing some movement between heel and ball of the foot.

Major sports shoe companies Nike and Asics made a major technological advance when they introduced air and gel into the midsoles. Nike devised pressurized air canals sealed within polyurethane (PU) and incorporated these into the heel and forefoot of the shoe. PU is a synthetic rubber that is firmer and more durable than EVA but has less cushioning. Asics introduced a silicone gel compound into an EVA foam midsole; the EVA is light, resilient and has good cushioning properties while the gel provides shock absorption.

Nike's air soles are an excellent shock absorber but do promote movability — which should be noted by runners requiring motion control. Asics' gel/EVA sole combines shock absorption with stability.

Outer Sole

The outer sole is that part of the shoe that comes into direct contact with the ground. Its prime function is for traction on running surfaces; it therefore needs to have good durability. It should not wear down too quickly, particularly at the outer heel edge. A certain degree of wear, however, is important in that it allows the shoe to mould gently to the foot strike pattern. Various adhesive substances and glues can be bought to patch the wearing down of shoes but generally an uneven outer sole means the end of a shoe's life span.

Orthotics

These are special custom-built inner soles that are specifically designed to cope with each runner's individual biomechanics. Worn inside the shoe they help to correct any running style fault the runner may have. Orthotics must be designed by a podiatrist or physiotherapist rather than bought over the counter in running stores. They do add weight to a shoe and can cause blisters, but generally they have proved useful for correcting specific running biomechanics in many runners.

Toe Box

The toe box of a shoe should be roomy and allow the toes to move fairly freely inside the shoe (test up-and-down movement). Avoid toe boxes made of hard plastic — this will guarantee black toenails and blisters. Test the amount of room in the toe area by measuring a thumb's-width or the width of your index finger between your longest toe and the front tip of the shoe.

RIGHT, TOP TO BOTTOM *The complex ridging on the outer sole of each shoe promotes good road traction; over-the-counter orthotics can help to correct a mildly pronating or supinating foot; the heel and forefoot component of a shoe showing the sealed air canals devised by Nike.*

Shoe last shapes

STRAIGHT   CURVED

MATCHING FOOT TYPE WITH SHOES

Pronators need to buy firm, supportive shoes with straight lasts and firm heel counters; these offer motion control. Their shoes must almost guide their feet out of the pronating posture and into the more bow-legged posture.

Of the shoe designs, these are the most inflexible, durable and therefore heavier. Features generally incorporated to create control are strengthened heel counters, extra medial (the inner shoe area under the foot arch) support, polyurethane or multidensity midsoles, and carbon-rubber outer soles.

Supinators, because of their high-arched feet, need the opposite, requiring shoes that have softer soles and contouring, and that allow them the freedom to pronate if there is such a tendency. A firm, supportive shoe would increase supination and could result in more injuries. The shoe design of this foot type usually features minimal medial support but extra cushioned midsoles for good shock absorption; this also encourages movement of the foot.

Neutral feet don't need any motion control features but best suit shoes designed for stability. These shoes usually offer a combination of durability, moderate cushioning, and some medial support or dual-density midsoles.

With experience and, initially, the help of knowledgeable shoe salespeople, runners will learn to better understand what foot type they are and therefore which shoes will be most suitable for them. Eventually they will also recognize which shoes are 'injury traps'. It is no coincidence that experienced runners often buy several pairs of a particular shoe because it serves them so well and because they fear it will go out of stock.

Tips for testing shoes

You need to arrive at the shoe store with the following kind of information to enable the shoe salesperson to correctly recommend a shoe type for you (and if it isn't asked of you, you should offer the information anyway!):

Your weight and height; how long you've been running for; what weekly distance you achieve; and whether you generally run on gravel, concrete or tar. It is an advantage to know whether you have a tendency to supinate or pronate, and if you've already been running for some time, bring along your existing pair of running shoes as this can help the salesperson to determine any wear in specific areas.

Otherwise, take note of the following tips:

▸ Feet swell during the day and particularly when you run, so it is best to try on shoes in the latter part of the day. It is not unusual for running shoes to be a half- or full size larger than your normal shoes.

▸ Wear socks when trying on the shoes.

▸ Test out both left and right shoes, as one foot is often slightly larger than the other (I suffer from this myself — my right foot is larger than my left).

▸ Make sure your heel is held snugly and does not slip out of the heel counter when you stride out.

CUSTOMIZING YOUR SHOES

Just because shoe manufacturers are able to incorporate wonderful technology into modern running shoes, creating masterpieces of design, does not mean they are perfect. The cost of running shoes may be off-putting, however experienced runners know that, if necessary, an expensive but ill-fitting shoe can be altered to become more corrective. If it is acceptable to put an orthotic in a shoe, why should it not also be acceptable to take a knife or a pair of scissors to your shoes in order to trim and alter them?

Runners who suffer excessively from blistered toes and black toenails may find it useful to cut away the toe box of a shoe. Certainly, runners in the past did this with less sophisticated shoes. The shoe can be cut with a sharp serrated knife at the join between the sole and the shoe fabric (see diagram). Surprisingly, an open toe box such as this does not result in stones entering the shoes — in fact, it allows mobile toes to expel the stones. These generally find their way into running shoes through the ankle and heel sections.

Some runners find that shoes with widely splayed heel wedges cause problems. The protruding edges of the wedges, too, can be trimmed with a sharp knife.

In addition, grooves can be cut widthwise across the underside of the sole of the shoe in order to create more 'give' and toe-off flexibility to the foot. If the soles are too rigid they can cause tendonitis and shin splints (see Injuries, p100) in the front lower leg or top of the foot.

Heel counter tabs, which occur at the back of the shoe and help to pull the shoe on, can also be trimmed off if they rub too vigorously against the Achilles tendon.

If the customizing is done correctly there should be little damage to the structure, cushioning and stability factors of the shoe. If you are in doubt, experiment with an old pair.

Customizing your shoes

Cutting Toebox

Trimming a heel wedge

Creating flexibility

RUNNER'S CLOTHING

Beginners don't at first realize how quickly heat is generated on a run as the circulatory system speeds up and the heart pumps blood to the surface of the body to lose that heat. In a process known as thermoregulation, the body works to maintain its ideal body temperature (around 37°C; 98.5°F); the more efficiently perspiration can evaporate, the less energy will be required by the body to regulate that temperature. The development of modern breathable fabrics, which also have wicking qualities that aid the removal and evaporation of sweat, improves the comfort of today's runners exercising in warm conditions.

For the warmer spring and summer months, all runners need wear is a pair of easy-fitting lightweight shorts and a running vest, loose-fitting sleeveless T-shirt or sports crop top. The best vests are of nylon mesh fabric, which promotes easy breathing of the skin. Tops should have wide armholes and minimal seams or labels which could cause chafing. Some shorts have a lining that absorbs sweat from the skin.

For the well-endowed women runners, bras designed with minimal stretch in the straps and front undersupport are best, particularly those whose straps meet at the back in a racer-back design, giving three-way support. Many women elect to wear a sports bra under a tight-fitting crop top for added control.

In winter it is best to wear several thin layers of clothing so that these can be removed and tied around the waist if you warm up sufficiently. The thin jackets of parachute-type fabric worn by kayakers are suitable, as they allow breathability but cut out a measure of wind chill and can be removed and folded into a tiny size. When conditions are both windy and wet, you should try to keep dry by wearing a Gore-Tex runner's jacket (this is a synthetic, waterproof fabric that allows the skin to breathe). For those whose hands suffer from the cold, a pair of inners of the type used by cricketers under their mitts serves this purpose well.

Running in subzero temperatures is a different matter. You will need a warm long-sleeved top or thermal jacket, long tights or track pants, and gloves. As a lot of heat is lost via the top of the head, a balaclava or woollen cap may also be necessary.

Socks

By far the majority of runners prefer wearing socks when they run. Even with modern running shoes, soft fabric sock-linings forming the inners to shoes can chafe, leading to the development of blisters. Socks help to absorb the sweat and act as an additional protective buffer against chafing.

Natural fibers such as 100 per cent cotton or cotton blends seem to protect the feet better; artificial fibers can burn and increase the risk of blisters (see also p55). Personally, I wear two pairs of natural-fiber socks, a thicker pair over a thin one. Certain manufacturers have designed socks that are padded to the underside to provide extra cushioning (see below), and the wicking-type material absorbs moisture from the feet to keep them cool and dry.

Always wear old worn-in socks for any important race or marathon; don't wear anything new. Socks that are fresh out of the packet may look good but may also be hazardous to the feet. Race in what you know feels comfortable.

Hats

Because of the tremendous amount of heat dispelled from the top of the head, it is foolish to wear a hat that traps the heat. Hats should ideally be a simple visor, offering protection to the eyes against the sun's glare but exposing the top of the head, thus allowing natural cooling.

Of course, not all of us are blessed with a head full of hair and we need to protect our heads from the harsh rays. A hat for this purpose should be perforated, which encourages air circulation.

The 1984 Olympic Marathon final in Los Angeles, was a fascinating race for a number of reasons, not least of which was that it pitted most of the world's greatest marathon runners against each other in the ultimate race for gold. It was also an exciting

spectacle because the race was run in the intense Californian heat and humidity. The different responses of the leading runners to the challenge of hot-weather distance running were interesting. A number thought that wearing hats would be an advantage (little did they realize that in the LA conditions only the correct style of hat would work).

Irishman John Treacy, Toshihiko Seko of Japan, and a number of other leading runners tossed their hats off almost without realizing it as the race progressed. With their brains literally beginning to stew, instinct kicked in, and one by one they removed the "pressure cookers" they had wrapped over their heads.

1 *A hat that exposes the top of the head (see bottom visor) is better than one that fully covers the head, as the latter traps an enormous amount of heat given off from this area of the body.*

2 *Because the top of the head is so vulnerable to heat loss, in cold climates that experience frost and snow it is often necessary to wear a woollen cap to protect the head and face.*

3 *Socks made of natural cotton fibers appear to be the best option for the prevention of blisters on runners' feet.*

4 *The racer-back bra (or crop top) has a solid triangular stretch of fabric to provide maximum three-way support for women runners.*

1

2

In certain weather conditions, clothing needs to insulate the body from the cold, while in others it needs to aid heat loss. In the former case, clothing serves to trap a thin layer of air against the body, which warms up to body temperature. Air does not conduct heat well, so this layer insulates the runner from further heat dissipation. In warm climates, where the loss of heat needs to be encouraged, light porous fabrics allow heat build-up and moisture to pass through the fabric and evaporate, thus keeping the runner cooler and drier.

1 Running vests of finely woven mesh offer 'breathability' and the easy dispersion of heat.

2 4 and **7** Long pants and jackets (some with hoods) of varying thicknesses are designed from new synthetic materials such as Gore-Tex and polypropylene which are relatively waterproof, repelling water while at the same time allowing the skin to breathe. Moisture build-up and sweat therefore don't accumulate on the skin, escaping instead into the air. Some clothing items have a wicking or mesh lining that absorbs moisture but doesn't retain it, thus it dries relatively quickly and helps the runner keep dry too.

3 These thin nylon sweatshirts are effective as windcheaters and also repel light rain. They are good against the early chill at the beginning of a run and because the fabric is so thin and lightweight, can be rolled up to fit into a runner's pouch or tied/wound around the waist when the runner is warmed up.

5 Crop tops and leggings from a cotton/Lycra blend are cool to run in, but remember that cotton is more moisture-absorbent than synthetics.

6 Lycra leggings are available in varying lengths: the elasticity of this synthetic fibre is good for the non-restrictive requirements of runners.

8 The synthetic fabrics and mesh linings of these lightweight shorts are effective in removing moisture from the body and speeding up evaporation.

5

6

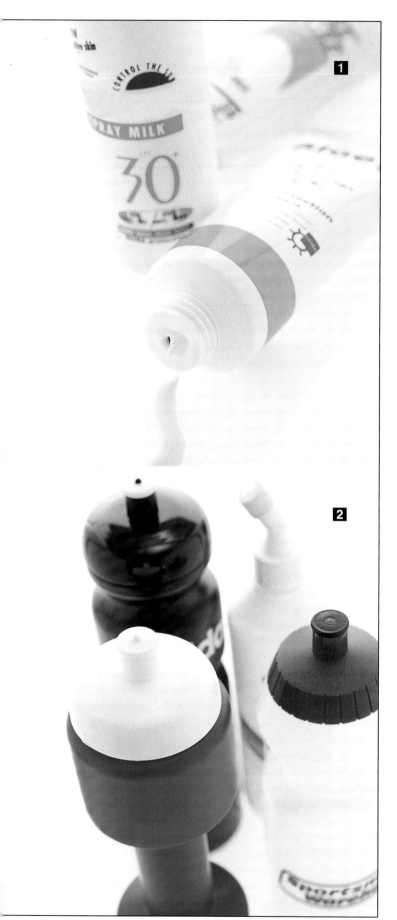

MISCELLANEOUS EQUIPMENT

Water Bottle

When setting out on longer runs along routes that do not have access to water — especially in hot conditions — it is advisable to carry a water bottle, which can also contain an isotonic drink. A variety of shapes designed for easy gripping while running is available from most sports shops.

Light for Night Running

The LED (Light Emitting Diode) lights used by cyclists are useful for runners who are on the road before dawn or after dusk, and some makes come attached to a strap that can be worn by the runner.

Runner's Belt

This is particularly useful for a long training run or race in which you may prefer to bring your own refreshments and supplements. Some belt designs can carry a water bottle and all have pockets and mesh compartments to store keys, gels and energy boosters.

Sun Protection

It is now widely recognized that the sun's rays can be very dangerous, particularly with today's increased ultraviolet radiation as a result of the atmosphere's depleted ozone layer, and skin cancer is a very real threat to anyone taking part in outdoor activities.

It is important to own a good sunblock cream of at least a 30 sun protection factor (SPF) — and make sure you use it! The cream should be water- and sweat-resistant but check that it does not irritate or sting the eyes.

Eyewear (and its Psychological Benefits)

For those who race seriously, sunglasses (see panel) help to disguise fatigue. Competing runners will often look into each other's eyes to gauge motivation and exhaustion, and possibly gain a psychological advantage over their competitors. A tired runner's eyes are dull and lifeless. Dark glasses — especially the reflective-type designs — project a strong, robot-like Darth Vader look and offer no glimpse into the "windows of the soul!"

Sunglasses, in cutting out harsh glare, also aid the relaxation of the face and muscles around the eyes as they aren't squinting into the sun. At the same time the neck muscles relax, as does the rest of the body, allowing you to run more efficiently.

1 *Because of the harm caused by overexposure to the sun, it is essential to use a sunscreen with a high SPF factor (at least SPF30).*

2 *A number of water-bottle design options offer ease of gripping while out on a training run — at bottom left is a handy dumbbell design.*

Protective eyewear

Because our eyes are exposed to the constant glare of the sun's ultraviolet (UV) radiation while out running, it is important to properly protect them. The ozone layer does filter out the C-type UV radiation, but not A- and B-type radiation. Extended exposure to these rays could create eye problems such as glaucoma (when increased pressure of the eyeball fluid damages the optic disc) and cataracts (opaqueness to the lens). New technology has ironed out many of the problems suffered by runners wearing sunglasses and over the years most manufacturers have introduced the following factors:

▸ Most lenses are designed to filter out 100 per cent UVA and UVB radiation

▸ Many lenses are manufactured from polycarbonate, which is scratch-resistant and shatterproof

▸ Different-colored lenses allow for various light conditions; some are interchangeable

▸ Thermogrip nosepads and nonslip rubber pads on the arms maintain a firm, snug grip with no slipping from sweat

▸ Some designs feature a lens that wraps around the face, cutting out glare from the sides

▸ Certain designs come with ventilation holes along the sides of the lenses to avoid any fogging up

Lens colors for different light conditions
▸ Blue, amber/brown and mirrored lenses: good for glare and bright sunlight

▸ Green and grey: suitable for all light conditions, from dim to full sun

▸ Yellow: used at night for dim conditions as it enhances the light that's available

3 *Runners' belts, besides being devised to carry all manner of personal effects, often feature reflective strips that are useful for night running.*

4 *This LED light on a strap is ideal for fixing around your waist to make yourself visible while out on a night run.*

5 *Most modern high-quality sunglasses are designed with rubberized special-grip arms, ventilation holes to prevent fogging and effective glare filters against bright sunlight.*

43

GETTING STARTED

THE RUNNER'S HIGH

Once you have made up your mind to start running, you need to promise yourself that you will give yourself the best chance of becoming a lifetime runner by committing to running four to five days a week for three months. If you succeed in keeping to this commitment, you will find that running soon becomes a regular part of your day.

We now know that the running or exercising body produces natural morphine-like hormones called endorphins which produce a pleasurable sensation that is sometimes referred to as the 'runner's high'. Endorphins are reputed to be natural pain relievers (playing a similar role to morphine) and create a satisfying feeling of well-being. The best way to experience a 'runner's high' is to abstain from running for two or three days; the first run after a lay-off produces a 'rush' of endorphins that leaves the body pleasantly sated from the exercise. It is a proven fact that beginners who have succeeded in running for up to three months, four to five days a week, find they are well and truly hooked and that they become irritable and ill at ease if they miss out on a run for too long.

THE CORRECT RUNNING STYLE

While there is no doubt that the world's greatest distance runners are also among the most efficient runners, correct running style and technique are not as important as they would be in a sport such as skiing or swimming. The important thing is to be as relaxed as possible and to concentrate on staying loose.

You should hold your torso upright, keeping your spine straight, and try not to run with the arms raised and moving from left to right across the chest, as this actually restricts your breathing. Tired runners tend to grit their teeth, clench their fists and tighten the neck muscles. The latter, in particular, is a clear sign of a straining runner. Many runners have a tendency, too, to hunch the shoulders. Train yourself in the beginning to focus on relaxing your posture; if you do find yourself raising your shoulders, borrow a visualization technique that is used in Yoga: imagine that mini-sandbags resting

LEFT *Scientific studies carried out on the gender differences between men and women — and how this influences their running — shows women to have double the body fat of men, and therefore less muscle mass, which may account for women not performing as well as men over long distances.*
RIGHT *When starting out with your running programme, stay as relaxed as possible, avoiding a hunched posture and tensed up shoulders. The aim is to achieve a certain efficiency in running, which requires less energy and effort.*

on them are weighing them down, thus encouraging you to relax them. A good time to focus on posture is while warming up at the beginning of a run or when winding down towards the end of a run.

The world's best sprinters concentrate on staying as relaxed as possible while sprinting flat-out. It is no coincidence that American Carl Lewis learned to sprint with open palms — it is hard to tense up when the hands are prevented from forming fists.

Successful distance runners also tend to exhibit as little vertical movement as possible, their head remaining almost on the same horizontal plane; that is, there is very little bobbing up and down (see diagram). Economy of movement is vital.

Learning to breathe correctly, too, is of great significance to runners. Beginners should train themselves, through becoming aware of their breathing, to inhale deeply from the base of the diaphragm, that is, from the pit of the stomach rather than from the upper chest (which tends to promote shallow breathing). Inhaling shallowly from the chest can result in a runner's stitch (see p52). It can take some time to perfect this method of breathing.

RIGHT *The USA's star track and field athlete, Carl Lewis, thrilled Americans in the 1984 Olympic Games held in Los Angeles when he won four gold medals, two of which were for the 100m and 200m track events. He was also declared the winner of the 100m in Seoul in 1988 after the controversial disqualification of Canadian Ben Johnson for drug-taking.*

Correct running style

An efficient runner creates very little bobbing movement of the head.

46

The above notwithstanding, it is obvious that style and technique are not always that important. American Alberto Salazar, a multiple marathon winner, has a very awkward, light running style; Emil Zatopek of Czechoslovakia won four distance running gold medals at the Olympic Games while appearing to run in agony all the way — head held stiffly to one side, and legs and arms flailing. Zola Budd, South African teenage wonder who rose to fame when she was only 18 years old, won two World Cross Country Championships barefoot (for the UK in 1985 and 1986), with her elbows stuck out awkwardly on both sides of her body.

GETTING OUT ON THE ROAD

Once first-time runners have decided to commit to some kind of training program, they should take note of the following advice.

Make it Very Easy

To begin with, run on flat, easy routes. Avoid big hills and keep the run relatively short. If possible, choose pleasant surroundings to run in; this makes it more tempting to run again. If you make it too hard too soon, you'll find a way to avoid running in no time.

Don't be Afraid to Walk

Don't chide yourself for walking, especially if a run is particularly arduous. Beginners should realize that it is perfectly acceptable to walk from time to time — in fact, there is a great deal of benefit to it. Many ultra-runners (those who run beyond 42km, or 26 miles) feel that an occasional walk during a race helps to relieve stiffness and aids recovery. It also temporarily reduces the constant impact of the road on the knees, and because walking uses different sets of muscles, the "running" leg muscles are given a rest.

Take heart, the best in the field resort to walking on occasions: Moroccan Brahim Boutayeb walked the last few paces of his Olympic 10,000m in Seoul in 1988, while American Bill Rodgers stopped to tie his shoe lace and to walk past a watering table (aid station) en route to winning his first Boston Marathon in 1975.

Don't Time your Runs

In doing so you create undue pressure for yourself. Many beginners want instant results and immediate improvement. Timing your early runs can become disappointing, as it is impossible to improve on every outing. A variety of reasons — from tiredness to weather conditions — can make it impossible to run well each time.

RIGHT *In the early stages of your running, don't make it hard for yourself by selecting difficult, hilly terrain to jog along; stay with the relatively flat easier courses until your fitness levels have increased.*

Run with a Friend

Running with a friend makes most runs a far more pleasurable experience than running alone (although some runners treat this as an opportunity for some 'time out' to spend on their own, alone with their thoughts).

Also, shared discipline is far easier to adhere to than individual discipline. There is more incentive to get out and run when you know that someone is waiting to meet up with you.

Do the Talk Test

Don't overdo your pace, initially. You should be able to talk to your fellow runner at virtually any point in a training run, with the possible exception of the steepest hills where breathing hard prohibits conversation. Talking while running is a great sign of good pace judgement.

Dress Lightly

Beginners are generally easy to spot because they are almost always overdressed. Bundled up in T-shirts and tracksuits on a warmish day, they forget that exercise generates a lot of heat. Light clothing is best in most situations; even in cold weather, the body warms up very quickly.

Don't Weigh Yourself

Those who hope to lose weight while running will be rewarded, but they need to allow the process time to work. Again, too many runners expect instant results and give up early because weight loss doesn't happen fast enough. Remember that the exercising body, in burning fat, is also busy building up muscle — which is heavier than fat. So for a while body mass can actually weigh more. However, one's body shape undeniably changes for the better.

Don't Race your Training Partner

Finally, try not to race your training partner. This can only make your runs hard and unpleasant as the one tries to keep up with the other. Always try to run shoulder to shoulder (unless in heavy traffic). There is nothing more irritating in running than a partner who insists on always being half a stride ahead. The time to race is in races; training partners should remember that no one can possibly be strong on every run.

BELOW *You may find that running with a companion will distract you from the initial exertion of exercise during the early days of your training, and sharing conversation will make the outdoor excursion pass by very quickly.*

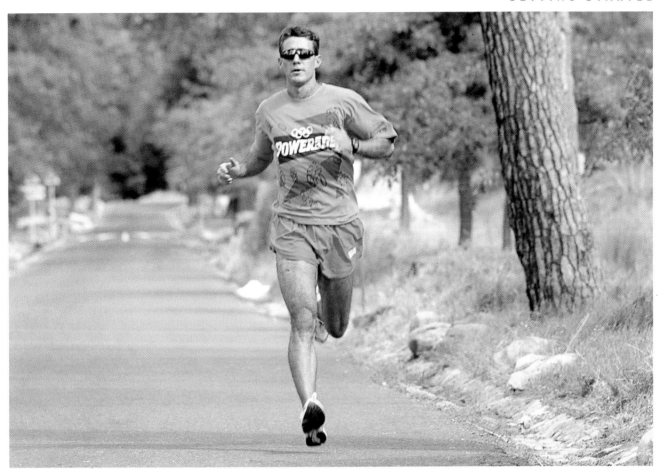

ABOVE *It is an undisputed fact that extended downhill running subjects the front thigh muscles (quadriceps) to intense pounding which in most cases leads to muscle damage. The only way to avoid this as much as possible is to do quadricep-strengthening exercises and added downhill training.*

TACKLING HILLS

Before beginners progress to hillier terrain, they should first feel comfortable on the flat, easy surfaces. The idea is for the fledgling runner to make early running as easy and as pleasant as possible so that he or she feels okay with the sport, and enjoys it. However, once runners are ready to tackle hills, they should be aware of how to economize on their hill running technique.

Maximizing Downhill Running

Take a lesson from the best downhill runners, who allow gravity to work for them and therefore suffer as little pounding and eccentric muscle contraction (see p24) as possible. Two good examples are American Bill Rodgers, who often breaks away from his opponents on steep downhills, and ultra-legend, South African Alan Robb, a four-times Comrades Marathon winner. Robb has a unique shuffle style that is very economical and results in his being very light on foot impact. His style is almost impossible to copy, but it is no coincidence that of the four Comrades Marathons he won, three were on the downhill route (from Pietermaritzburg to Durban – run in alternate years). Gravity works for the runners here, some of whom run in a seemingly uncontrolled, loose-limbed style to the bottom of the hills. Athletes who are not good downhill runners tend to lean backwards and resist the gravitational pull. Generally, they will pound the ground more and suffer more muscle damage on the very steep descents.

Maximizing Uphill Running

The best uphill runners lean into a hill and almost tug their way up, as if pulling on an imaginary rope (this is the technique promoted by famous Boston coach Bill Squires of the Greater Boston Track Club, who was also the coach for Bill Rodgers). American Chuck Smead, multiple winner of hill races, had his uphill running technique honed to pull him rapidly away from the competition. The secret to maximizing your progress on uphills is that on getting to the top, you should push on over and keep going beyond the crest of the hill. Too many runners ease up as the summit approaches.

49

THE IMPORTANCE OF KEEPING A RUNNING DIARY

If running shoes are the most important item in a runner's life, then keeping a logbook or training diary must be the next in line. Certainly I feel that a training diary is indispensable although sadly for too many runners it is not. Many of them fail to see any merits in keeping a logbook as the general idea is that if one just does the training, the results will follow.

However, the advantages are simply too many to ignore and the few minutes spent filling in a log really can save hours of wasted training on the road.

ADVANTAGES

Tracks Progress

A training diary allows runners to keep track of their progress. From the data one can see fitness improve, record a series of carefully planned training sessions, and check whether a previously successful important session or training method has been missed or overlooked when trying to repeat the performance.

Acts as a Source of Reference

The logged information can be looked at historically. Even if entries seem random at first, you will see patterns emerge later. By referring back to old training diaries, you can repeat training patterns that proved successful or work on past mistakes and correct them. Without this approach, it is almost impossible to be truly scientific about one's training.

Good Motivation

Surprisingly, training diaries can motivate as well as provide a log. Nothing can be more motivating to a runner than the conscious monitoring of his or her progress by recording it in writing. Those with ambition and drive in life often write their goals down. Similarly, a runner's diary is a recorded progress chart in which you can watch running times improve, body weight reduce and that important red-ringed date — 'race day' — draw nearer!

No two runners will keep the same training diaries, nor will they record the same information, but there is certain key information that must be included, for example, length of run, time taken to complete the run (although beginners may want to ignore this at first), difficulty of the course, time of day and weather conditions (it is a fact that strong headwinds, for example, or an intensely hot day will affect performance). Of lesser importance but still relevant, training companions can be recorded, as can pulse rates and the model of training shoes worn — the latter to gauge whether a particular brand is suitable for you or causes any discomfort. Runners

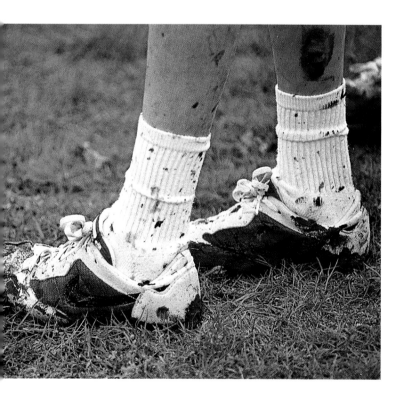

ABOVE AND LEFT *The information you record in your running diary can cover everything from your heart rate registered over a particular run to what brand of shoes you wore or how the weather conditions affected your run.*

are free to record as much or as little information as they want. Races participated in should be recorded in detail with observations about key times during the race or 'splits' (see p79) at vital points, tactics used, and your racing competitors. Again, climate, head-winds, and so on should be included.

Book stores carry specially devised running diaries but they can just as easily be created out of a simple blank or ruled notebook.

All of the information combined becomes a personal reference book which, after a few years, is almost like a personal running encyclopaedia and becomes a valuable weapon in the pursuit of faster times and improved fitness.

BE AWARE

Don't be Controlled by your Diary

You should guard against running purely for your diary. It is important to understand that you will need to be flexible and allow for rest days, and those bad and demotivated days.

Just because you ran 160km (100 miles) over a calendar week two years ago shortly before your favourite race doesn't mean you have to do it again, at all costs. The diary can indeed help you to try to duplicate an old successful training programme — but not with a rigid, inflexible approach.

Avoid Keeping a Diary for the Wrong Reasons

It is important to avoid believing that 'more is better'. If you ran well last year, doing more training does not necessarily mean you will run better this year, and you should avoid keeping a training log for this purpose.

The logbook is used preferably to correct mistakes or improve weaknesses. For example, in a previous year's race you may have noticed a weakness on some of the hills. Looking back through your diary you see that most of your training routes were on flat courses. You can decide, therefore, to train on hillier courses this year to iron out that weakness.

Of the many benefits of keeping a training diary, the most important one is that it avoids the 'hit and miss' angle, ensuring a correct scientific approach for any serious runner.

Too many runners have great races and are then unable to duplicate them or, for that matter, improve, one of the chief reasons being that they have no written record of their build-up to a particularly successful race.

RIGHT *Your training companions could also find themselves logged in your diary — or even a running opponent against whom you may need to devise special tactics for a particular race in which you are both participating.*

RUNNERS' HAZARDS

Although the following list of less-serious runner's injuries is encountered by most runners at one time or another, beginners to the sport are more prone to these due to a degree of unfitness, inexperience and not yet being tuned to their bodies.

THE RUNNER'S STITCH

Sooner or later every runner will experience a 'stitch'. It does appear to occur most commonly in beginners and there is some debate as to what causes it. However, there is no debate that a stitch can be very painful: it is a sharp pain in the side or diaphragm, or beneath the rib cage. A severe stitch can bring a runner to a halt, which is critical in a major race. What occurs is that the bouncing action of running disturbs the stomach, liver and spleen, which are attached to the same ligaments as the diaphragm. Creating tension, the diaphragm contracts, causing the acute pain of the stitch.

Don Kardong of the USA, who was placed fourth in the 1976 Olympic Marathon in Montreal, Canada, suffered from stitches; he believed that if he cut out green vegetables from his diet in the days prior to a race, this helped prevent its onset. Some runners believe milk products can cause gas build-up, and as a result, cramps and a stitch. The urge for a pitstop, too, can bring on the characteristic sharp pain. Personally, I am convinced that stitches are caused by tense runners. Running stiffly and in a slightly unusual style can tense up the diaphragm.

To relieve the pain, you should change your running style by shortening the stride and altering your breathing pattern; drop your arms to your sides and try taking deeper, slower breaths on both the intake and outtake of breath. Pressing your fingers firmly into the ribs where the pain is located does provide some relief and may help to stimulate relaxation of the constricted muscle, as does lifting the arm on the side of the stitch, again to relax the diaphragm. It is best to try to run through a stitch.

CRAMPS AND THEIR CAUSES

Scientists and physiologists are uncertain of what actually causes cramping during long distance running, but it remains the bane of runners. Striking savagely, often without warning, a cramp can bring a runner to an agonizing, grinding halt. These contractions most frequently attack the hardest-working muscles — the quadriceps (front of the thighs), the calf muscles, and the hamstrings.

LEFT *Larger, well organized races often have trained medical staff stationed along particular sections of the race route to provide relief to runners for chafing and blisters, and to massage cramped muscles.*

Electrolyte imbalance Some runners believe that an electrolyte, or mineral imbalance, is the cause of cramps, however there is no real proof of this. Generally, runners do tend to take extra calcium, magnesium, potassium, and sodium (salt) to ward off muscle seizures. Such trace elements are essential (although in small doses) for the correct functioning of body metabolism and the muscles. Magnesium and potassium aid the ability to exercise; the latter is stored together with glycogen, which is the energy source for all muscular work. Calcium strengthens the bones through calcification while sodium, stored in the body fluids, maintains the balance of water throughout the body, influences blood pressure and is also present in the muscular process.

It may help to take these minerals as part of your daily diet, but they should not be ingested specifically before or during a race because in many cases, particularly in the dehydrating body, the concentration of minerals in the individual cells increases as they lose fluid. A high intake of magnesium, for instance, can lead to stomach problems like diarrhoea.

There is a theory, too, that ingesting salt drinks will ease cramps. However, it is generally believed that most Western diets already contain too much salt without a need for adding any; and studies show that the loss of salt through sweating is marginal, even during hard running (also, salt loss decreases the fitter you are).

Temperature and dehydration The day's temperature and dehydration in the runner could influence the onset of cramps as there seems to be a definite connection between the three factors — experienced distance runners frequently complain that cramps become more of a problem under these conditions. In hot weather, the body cools by pumping blood to the surface of the skin in an effort to lose heat; this happens first through convection (transfer from a hotter to a cooler zone) and then through the production of sweat. Fluids are lost through sweat, leading to dehydration. The solution appears to be to drink refrigerated fluids before the run and/or in the beginning stages of a run to hydrate the muscles well and at the same time regulate their temperature, and to moderate one's pace and effort for the tougher conditions.

Length and distance The prime causes of cramping are now considered to be time and sheer distance. These are linked to genetic factors that almost preordain when a runner will cramp. It appears that in a limited but frequent range of movement requiring great effort, a point will be reached where the muscle simply rebels against the work and seizes up; the signals to contract and relax become confused and the muscle goes rigid. It is believed that for each particular runner there is a point at which he or she will cramp — and that is genetically inherited.

How to Combat Cramps

Experienced runners fight a cramp while running by changing their running style and adjusting their effort. While cramps sometimes come on as an unpleasant shock, there can be warning signals; this can be a tickling, trickling sensation in the muscle or a slight tightening, tug or ache. A runner can delay the full cramp by slowing down, and by running slightly pigeon-toed or duck-footed. Shortening the stride — or even lengthening it on downhills — may also help. Many runners try to resist the urge to come to a grinding halt as this often heralds the onset of major cramps.

If forced to stop, however, runners should try to gently stretch out the cramping muscle. Try leaning against a lamp post or tree and very slowly straighten the legs. Massage the cramp by kneading it with the fingers. Muscles that have started the cramping process often cramp again, so begin running at a slow, easy pace that gradually eases the muscle back to work.

At no stage should a runner force or run through a cramp, as it can lead to a tear, and bleeding within the muscle, which could take a long time to heal.

BELOW *Race participants can prepare for potential problems before a race by massaging muscle relaxants into problem zones and bandaging blister-prone areas with adhesive strips.*

Stretching

Making a habit of stretching before and after a race may also help to relieve cramps since muscle that has a greater range of movement will resist the onset of contractions. There are, however, many runners who believe that stretching can, in fact, injure distance runners, doing more harm than good. While stretching used to be a fashionable addition to running — particularly before an excursion — it has become less so today (see panel).

CHAFING

Most runners will experience some form of chafing, caused by friction of the skin when body parts rub together, removing the protective outer skin layer, or epidermis, thus exposing the inner layer, or dermis. This condition is very sensitive during showering or bathing and can be very uncomfortable. Areas commonly affected are between the thighs, the outer part of the underarms, wherever clothing seams of tight-fitting crop tops or sports bras chafe the

The case for stretching

Recent studies have cast doubt on the efficacy of stretching before running a race, and there is now some support for the idea that there is little benefit to be had from it. Certainly athletes like the great Australian marathoner Robert de Castella do not believe in stretching; he and runners like him believe that this actually increases the incidence of injury. For them, the best approach to ensuring that muscles are loose and warm for running is to run a couple of gentle kilometres at a very slow pace before gradually increasing the tempo.

Those runners who prefer stretching (and there are still many) argue that the relatively limited range of movement in running results in shortened, tight muscles and tendons, particularly those at the back of the leg such as the hamstrings, calf muscles, and Achilles tendon. They believe that a runner should spend 10 to 15 minutes stretching — which lengthens the muscles — before running, particularly before any fast running or racing. Such runners refute the stretching-induced injury theory, believing that the injuries are a result of incorrect stretching techniques having been practised rather than the act of stretching itself. Advocates of stretching recommend that each muscle stretch should be held gently, just before the point of pain, for at least 30 seconds.

The practice of Yoga, which puts great emphasis on the virtues of stretching, employs the theory that the ultimate benefit is received by holding a position for 60 seconds, or more, as this sends a firm message to the brain via the nerve centres to lengthen the muscle to its fullest extent. No stretch should be forced and it should never be done in a bouncing, jerky manner. This merely serves to shorten the muscle, which is what you are trying to counteract in a stretch. (See stretches and weight-lifting exercises on p72.)

skin, where sunglasses rest over the ears, and men, particularly, suffer friction of the nipples. Women are generally protected from the latter condition because of the bras and sports tops they wear. Labels in clothing can also cause chafing, so it is better to cut these off where they are likely to irritate the skin.

Prevention

Chafing can be prevented by applying Vaseline (the most popular product), anti-chafe cream or sports lubricant to the areas exposed to friction. To protect the nipples, runners apply a small strip of Elastoplast or any sticky adhesive tape that will hold to the skin when damp or wet. Where the feet are concerned, many experienced runners advise against applying lubricants to this area as it tends to increase movement and exacerbate rather than prevent rubbing and blisters.

BLISTERS

Although one can hardly take blisters seriously when matched against muscle strains, pulled tendons and other such injuries, no-one can ignore that they are extremely painful. Caused by constant pressure and rubbing mainly of the toes and feet, they are the result of fluid accumulating beneath the skin which creates a protective cushion over the irritated area. Blood blisters occur when tiny blood vessels burst during the rubbing. When these puncture, there is a possibility of an infection if bacteria penetrate the area.

The major causes of blisters are ill-fitting running shoes or an incorrect choice of footwear. Too-tight shoes will force toenails to constantly hit the toe box, while shoes that are too big will have your foot sliding around, creating friction and therefore blisters. During a race, the feet swell more from heat build-up, sweat and the added moisture from the water that runners pour over themselves at

watering tables, so they are more prone than usual to the forming of blisters. Socks should fit snugly with no wrinkles and without bunching up at the heels or toes.

Sports doctors suggest leaving the smaller, more harmless blisters as these will dry out on their own, but recommend puncturing the larger ones since these tend to be uncomfortable and painful when pressure is applied to them. This is done using a needle that has been sterilized with alcohol and draining the liquid by swabbing it with a piece of cottonwool. Apply an adhesive plaster to protect the blister and keep it free of bacteria.

Prevention

Some suggested preventive measures against blisters are to wear socks of a natural-blend cotton-fibre and synthetic fabric that are absorbent and draw moisture away from the feet. Reinforced toes and heels help to hold the sock snugly.

Many runners wear two pairs of socks, a thinner inner pair and thicker outer pair, so that any friction occurs between the socks rather than between skin and fabric.

If you know which areas of your foot are susceptible to blisters, you can, before setting out on a run, apply lengths of adhesive strip to those spots to protect them from chafing.

Some runners do advocate lubricating sensitive areas with Vaseline; others even apply a lubricant between their toes — but be very wary of friction and increased movement since this is what causes blisters to form in the first place!

BELOW *Blisters may seem like a relatively harmless irritation but all runners will confirm that they can cause excruciating pain. Preventive measures include wearing two pairs of socks — a thicker pair over a thinner one — or applying adhesive strips over areas that tend to chafe.*

THE DREADED PIT STOP

Most runners will have a horror story to tell about personal experiences of the 'runner's trots' — or simply the need for an urgent pit stop while on an informal run or during a race. Evidence indicates that this condition does not occur in cyclists or swimmers but is confined, rather, to the running fraternity. The constant bobbing up and down of the runner causes a great amount of upheaval in the stomach, in the least case precipitating natural bowel movement but more frequently upsetting the stomach sufficiently to bring on cramping and diarrhoea. It is believed that this may also be influenced by an increase in hormone concentrations in the blood. Sports scientist Tim Noakes, co-founder of the Sports Science Institute of South Africa, whose famous tome *Lore of Running* is often referred to as 'the runner's bible', puts forward the theory that 'runner's trots' is in many cases caused by a mild intolerance to dairy products or certain foods. Studies have proved that in certain runners, cutting dairy products from their diet has completely cured them of cramping and diarrhoea.

Prevention

For those runners who are aware that they have a dairy or milk intolerance, it is advisable not to ingest milk products for at least 24 hours before running a race. Another option is to avoid high-fibre meals that contain a lot of roughage 24 hours beforehand, and rather to eat highly refined foods with a high energy content, thus limiting the likelihood of a pit stop during the run.

If beginner runners find that they regularly experience the need for a pit stop during their informal runs, it is sometimes wise to devise a two-looped route that has one of its loops running past their home, or to find a route that runs past a vehicle service station with facilities.

YOU WILL NOT RUN YOUR BEST LONG-DISTANCE RACE AT YOUR FIRST ATTEMPT; REMEMBER THAT NOTHING REPLACES CONSISTENT WEEKS, MONTHS AND YEARS OF TRAINING.

WOMEN RUNNERS AND PERSONAL SAFETY

It is an unfortunate fact that women are more prone to attack than men. However, it is also not always possible to find a friend or training partner to run with who can fit in with your running schedule. In the absence of a running partner, women should heed the following advice when setting out alone:

▸ Choose routes through suburban or high density areas

▸ Don't run after dark

▸ Be constantly aware of your surroundings and people in front of or behind you

▸ If there is a suspect-looking individual ahead or nearby, cross the street or road

▸ Carry a protective device such as a whistle or personal alarm

▸ If you do run in a park, forest or undeveloped natural area, do so only with a companion

▸ If you get into the unfortunate positon of being accosted, try to startle your attacker by screaming loudly and if you are able to, fight back strongly. Try to jab your attacker's vulnerable areas, such as the eyes, the throat, the solar plexus or the groin, with your fingers, elbow or knee.

JOINING A RUNNING CLUB

Of the several advantages there are in joining a running club, a major reason runners consider it is to secure a permanent annual licence number. Most road races organized by formal athletics or road running associations require entrants to pay for and wear a temporary licence number (if they do not have their own official number) for the duration of the race. Registering with a club is generally more cost-effective than continually paying for such temporary numbers. Not all countries make use of a permanent licence number, such as the UK, for example, where those who are

LEFT AND FAR LEFT *Jogging with others in forested or high foliage areas promotes greater safety. If you insist on running on your own, carry a small defence spray (note: this is illegal in certain countries) or, alternatively, a whistle or personal alarm which draws attention by emitting an ear-splitting sound.*

not members of an affiliated club are required instead to pay a higher race entry fee. Club regulations also generally stipulate that members wear vests and shorts in club colours for all official races, so you need to be prepared to buy new running gear. In addition, there is an annual fee.

Most clubs are happy to allow prospective members to join them on a free trial evening run to ascertain whether the atmosphere and club spirit suits them. One great advantage of being a club member is that the club will hold regular evening runs of variable distances and catering to runners of varying fitness levels, as well as timed trials to monitor speed improvement among individuals, and longer weekend runs. This is especially useful when runners start training for specific races and need to challenge themselves over longer distances under controlled conditions (on weekend club runs, participants contribute a small fee and volunteers supply water, soft drinks or other refreshments along the route).

Undoubtedly the best part of joining a running club is the camaraderie and support you experience. You will be surprised how many spectators along a race route, on recognizing your club colours, will loudly cheer you along. And on particularly taxing runs — especially when you're running far from home or in unfamiliar territory — you will find that members of your own club (whether you know them personally or not) will acknowledge you and encourage you to keep going whenever they pass you along the route.

A club is also a source for training partners, advice from the more experienced runners and shared lifts to official races. Club tents at race venues allow you to meet up with fellow club members, with whom you can celebrate or commiserate, share your triumphs or ordeals.

It allows you, too, to find runners of varying ability with which to share your training schedule — be it speed trials, paced weeknight sessions or relaxed, longer weekend runs.

To find out about the local running clubs in your area, ask at your nearest sports shop, call the sports desk at your local newspaper or consult your telephone directory for local athletics associations who can direct you further. Running magazines are also a good source of information, and most national federations have a directory of athletic clubs on their website, which will lead you to the websites of the individual clubs.

YOUR FIRST 10K RACE

DEFINING FITNESS

For most runners, levels of fitness are fairly easy to guess, just as we know when we are poorly trained. Our body shape reminds us; our guilt over recently missed training tells us; as does the first decent climb on a training run. In many ways distance running is one of the most honest and predictable of all sports. We have all heard the stories of golfers who have not played golf in ages and yet who shoot a great round; and if you're in the right place at the right time in a football match, you too can score the winning goal despite being very unfit. But in running, if you haven't done the training, you will soon find out. Battling up a hill your heart will pound and your legs will feel heavy and tired; your lungs will burn and you may even cough and taste the metallic hint of blood.

The signs of poor fitness are very different from those of the overtrained, tired, or even slightly ill (yet fit) runner. These athletes experience the odd bad day and may struggle from time to time, but they have a central core of fitness, a residual strength that always surfaces. Sort out the illness, have a good night's sleep or even take a day off — and the running will bounce back. If you are not fit, however, no amount of rest or sleep can hide the fact.

PROFILE OF A FIT RUNNER

The fit runner knows it once he or she has attained that state of fitness. A spring in the stride and a joy to the running is evident in hands and arms being carried confidently, head up, chin vertical (an unfit runner's chin is often slumped towards the chest and his or her hands are tight fists of discomfort). Fit runners look forward to a run, and enjoy the experience of being in the outdoors. If hills still hurt, it is only because the runners intentionally attack the hill; they breathe hard but only because they choose to, not because they are forced to. The metabolism of well-trained runners drives them, often making them appear busy and fidgety. Sleep comes easily to them but they are quick to get up when sleep is over. The entire body functions well, from posture to circulation and the digestive system. When all these physical signs come together the fit runner feels on top of the world, and has a keen interest in completing the race he or she has trained so hard for.

Recognizing your own fitness levels

Less experienced runners may need some ways of measuring fitness. The following factors are a good way to monitor a body whose fitness is increasing.

Weight loss The first sign may be a dramatic loss in weight. Be aware, however, that weight loss can take some time and the fat that is burned away is replaced by leaner muscle tissue — but muscle is of course heavier than fat, so the scales may actually tell a depressing story. After weeks of running your weight may have gone up. The reality, though, is that your shape will have improved — you will be leaner and more muscular. When elite athletes start to get superfit, weight loss can be very dramatic and can continue despite increased food intake.

TOP *Being in the company of large numbers of runners who are feeling the same way as you — added to the charged atmosphere of a race — can be very motivating to a fledgling runner.*

RIGHT *On a sweltering day, well-known South African runner Desmond Zibi sprays himself with one of the water sachets handed out at supportive watering tables lining the route to cool himself during a race.*

CONSISTENCY ENABLES US TO STEP UP OUR TRAINING MILEAGE SUDDENLY, TO COPE PHYSICALLY WITH A LONG WEEKEND RUN AND TRAIN AGAIN THE NEXT DAY, AND TO QUICKLY REGAIN FITNESS WHEN INJURY STRIKES.

Improved health and sleep patterns   A fit runner rarely has to count sheep! REM (rapid eye movement) sleep — which is that portion of the sleep process during which we have our most vivid dreams and is the most positive and restorative for our bodies — is prolonged and deeper than normal. Digestive problems and constipation are absent and sexual interest is healthy. The fact that the whole body functions well as a result of being put through its paces proves that it is designed to be used and exercised, not rested and saved, and that it rewards those who use it sensibly.

Monitoring heart/pulse rate   Most runners are aware that they can measure their fitness levels by recording their heart/pulse rate. This is at its lowest first thing in the morning and it increases as the day progresses; from resting to exercise, the pulse rises by about 10 beats per minute. A generally low pulse rate is an indication of fitness, but a better indication of a fit state is the speed with which that pulse rate, pushed to its maximum, returns to resting level. Recovery is the key. When a runner is fit, he/she will find his or her pulse rate recovering very quickly from its maximum level. In the case of the unfit runner, the pulse rate will still be elevated several minutes after easing off from the exercise.

Your pulse usually beats more firmly in the little hollow below the mound where the outer edge of the thumb joins the wrist. To feel the pulse, press here lightly with your finger and measure the beats for 15 seconds, then multiply by four to get your heart rate. (Some running literature suggests counting for 10 seconds and multiplying by six, but when your pulse is racing it is harder to count the beats.)

HEART MONITORS

Thanks to modern technology, the heart monitor has helped thousand of runners, cyclists and triathletes improve their understanding of the fitness process. A transmitter in the form of a band that is held snugly and comfortably around the chest constantly monitors the runner's heart rate, and the reading is transmitted to a wrist watch which can be programmed to give audible signals (beeps or rings) to indicate certain target pulses.

LEFT AND OPPOSITE *Many leading sports manufacturers are now producing their own versions of the heart monitor, a transmitter that is electromagnetically linked via radio frequency to a wrist watch. The watch stores information that can later be downloaded onto a personal computer and analyzed. A heart monitor is a very useful item of equipment during training as runners can check their heart rate at the end of a difficult section and monitor how rapidly the heart recovers once they have completed a recovery lap. When doing interval training, their intervals can also be recorded on the watch as laps, each one being logged with its attendant heart rate and spot time.*

The heart rate monitor enables runs to be maintained at certain pulse rates and can signal a warning when the maximum effort is reached. In particular, the heart monitor reflects your progress in your efforts to become fitter. Because there is a direct link between heart rate and the amount of oxygen being taken in, runners can judge their oxygen consumption vs their running effort. Note that endurance running and the day's temperature do have a marked effect on heart rate. After a normal one-hour run, your heart could be pumping 20 beats faster per minute; and if the day is 10°C (50°F) hotter than usual, your heart rate may be 10 beats per minute higher than it would be on a cooler day.

The intensity of the different types of running discussed later is measured as a percentage of a runner's maximum heart rate. For a general idea, this rate is 200 beats/minute for athletes aged 20–29, and 190 beats/minute for those between 30 and 39.

If you want to get a more accurate measurement of your maximum heart rate, try a tip out of the monthly publication *Runner's World*: run 1km (½ a mile) at a steady pace, rest for two minutes, then run 1km at your fastest speed. Measure your pulse rate at the end of this for your maximum heart rate.

To test your fitness over time using a heart monitor, find a straight stretch near your home of around 1000m (1010yd). Run it at a comfortable pace and at the end record your heart rate and the time it took. Repeat this exercise over several weeks of training, and you should see a drop in both heart rate and the time taken to complete the stretch.

Many experienced runners see the training process and their training runs as a science — in their efforts to create a fit, racing body. There is a great need for the heart monitor in this case. However, runners should guard against becoming too reliant on this device in a racing situation. At this stage, running becomes an art form. Racing athletes need to respond to surges, and to tactics. A lot of racing is instinctive and intuitive, and runners need to run according to how they feel. In this arena, the heart monitor can stifle creativity and be a hindrance rather than a help. It is an extremely useful running aid, but understand that it is neither a coach nor a psychologist.

UNDERSTANDING VO$_2$ MAX

It is possible, in a laboratory, to measure fitness in a treadmill test known as the VO$_2$ max. This measures the maximum amount of oxygen that an individual can take in, in relation to body weight, during his or her highest exercise effort; this effort can only be sustained for between five and 10 minutes. (Do bear in mind that VO$_2$ max figures may vary from one laboratory to another depending on the procedures used.) The VO$_2$ max of a number of past elite runners is: Sebastian Coe (83), Bruce Fordyce (75), and Frank Shorter

(72). It is quite a lengthy and expensive procedure (as well as being gruelling and unpleasant) and requires expert assistance. For this reason, most runners will never bother to have a VO$_2$ max test; elite runners, however, find the procedure informative.

Take note, though, that the test can be psychologically damaging because it is a shatterer of dreams. You cannot escape the fact that VO$_2$ max is genetic and inherited. Training and weight loss can improve the result somewhat but essentially a world-class VO$_2$ max has to be in your genes.

To do the test, the participant runs on a treadmill which gradually builds his or her pulse rate up to the maximum (between 180 and 220 beats per minute) and the oxygen uptake is measured over a minute. The average person has an oxygen uptake in the region of 55, elite athletes have readings close to 80. Despite this, some runners are still able to perform with a relatively low VO_2 max. The USA's Frank Shorter had a lowish VO_2 max — by elite standards — yet he was still able to win the Olympic Marathon in Munich, Germany, in 1972. Generally, though, with a low VO_2 max it is impossible to be a world-class athlete.

However, it is also possible to train your muscles to use up the oxygen present more effectively, and you do this first by identifying your own VO_2 max and the speed at which it is reached, then training once a week at this pace — thus teaching the muscles to increase oxygen uptake. According to sports scientist Tim Noakes, VO_2 pace, rather than being an all-out sprint is actually a tempo run you are able to maintain over 10–21km (6–13 miles). By running 5–8km (3–5 miles) at 85 per cent VO_2 max once a week, you can shift your lactate turnpoint to a higher percentage VO_2 max — that is, increase the uptake of oxygen and at the same time extend the period before your muscle efficiency starts dropping. See also lactate on p118. The benefit of high-intensity workouts is that they enhance the heart's ability to supply oxygen and the muscles' ability to use that oxygen to clear lactate from the blood. And by extending your lactate turnpoint, you are able to run faster for longer. If you are able to locate a track at a school or sports complex, try out the following workout at your personal VO_2 max rate:

800m (880yd) at 3–6 repeats with a 2–3-minute recovery jog in-between each repeat

or

400m (440yd) at 8–12 repeats with a 2–3-minute recovery jog in-between

Predicted paces over various distances for your personal VO_2 max

VO_2 MAX VALUE	5KM (3 MILES)	10KM (6 MILES)	21.1KM (13 MILES)	30KM (18 MILES)	42.2KM (26 MILES)	56KM (35 MILES)
82.4	13:00	27:01	59:25	1:26:32	2:04:31	2:47:55
75.5	14:00	29:04	1:04:02	1:33:16	2:14:09	3:00:44
69.7	15:00	31:08	1:08:40	1:40:02	2:23:47	3:13:31
64.6	16:00	33:12	1:13:19	1:46:48	2:33:25	3:26:16
60.2	17:00	35:17	1:17:58	1:53:35	2:43:01	3:38:57
56.3	18:00	37:21	1:22:38	2:00:21	2:52:34	3:51:34
52.8	19:00	39:26	1:27:19	2:07:06	3:02:06	4:04:08
49.7	20:00	41:31	1:31:59	2:13:51	3:11:35	4:16:37
47.0	21:00	43:36	1:36:36	2:20:34	3:21:00	4:29:01
44.5	22:00	45:41	1:41:18	2:27:15	3:30:23	4:41:21
42.2	23:00	47:46	1:45:57	2:33:54	3:39:42	4:53:36
40.1	24:00	49:51	1:50:34	2:40:32	3:48:57	5:05:47
38.3	25:00	51:56	1:55:11	2:47:07	3:58:08	5:17:52
36.5	26:00	54:00	1:59:46	2:53:39	4:07:16	5:29:52
35.0	27:00	56:04	2:04:20	3:00:09	4:16:19	5:41:47
33.5	28:00	58:08	2:08:53	3:06:37	4:25:19	5:53:37
32.2	29:00	1:00:12	2:13:24	3:13:01	4:34:14	6:05:22
30.9	30:00	1:02:15	2:17:53	3:19:23	4:43:06	6:17:01

Reprinted from *Lore of Running* with kind permission: Tim Noakes and Oxford University Press

Pacing table

YOUR 10K TIME (MINUTES)	YOUR MAX VO$_2$ PACE (MIN/KM)	YOUR LACTATE THRESHOLD PACE (MIN/KM)	YOUR RUNNING ECONOMY PACE (MIN/KM)
27	2:34	2:55	3:37
28	2:39	3:01	3:46
29	2:45	3:08	3:53
30	2:50	3:14	4:00
31	2:55	3:20	4:09
32	3:00	3:26	4:16
33	3:05	3:32	4:23
34	3:11	3:38	4:32
35	3:16	3:44	4:39
36	3:22	3:51	4:46
37	3:27	3:57	4:54
38	3:32	4:03	5:01
39	3:37	4:09	5:09
40	3:43	4:15	5:16
41	3:49	4:21	5:24
42	3:54	4:27	5:31
43	3:59	4:33	5:38
44	4:04	4:39	5:45
45	4:10	4:45	5:53
46	4:15	4:51	6:00
47	4:20	4:57	6:07
48	4:25	5:03	6:14
49	4:30	5:08	6:22
50	4:36	5:14	6:28
51	4:41	5:20	6:35
52	4:46	5:26	6:43
53	4:51	5:32	6:50
54	4:56	5:38	6:56
55	5:02	5:44	7:03
56	5:07	5:49	7:10
57	5:12	5:55	7:17
58	5:18	6:01	7:24
59	5:23	6:07	7:31
60	5:27	6:13	7:31

Reprinted with kind permission: Joe Henderson, *Runner's World*

Runners can improve their running by focusing on improving their VO_2 max through training (as discussed on p62); by lengthening — also through training — the point at which their muscles stop working at optimum levels (i.e. lactate turnpoint); and by doing more endurance running to improve what's called running economy.

Extending your Lactate Turnpoint

The longer the muscles can work before becoming fatigued the better your performance. Your lactate turnpoint is calculated as 85 per cent of VO_2 max and in terms of running speed is only slightly faster than your marathon pace. Run for 5–10km (3–6 miles) at this pace as a workout, or incorporate it into a longer run.

Running Economy

This term refers to running at a pace that is easy but is still beneficial to your training. Most people will run too fast for the correct running economy pace — but don't make it too slow either. It can be calculated at 65 per cent of VO_2 max. Essentially this pace allows your body to get used to being on the road for a few hours, and should be attempted on your one long distance run (which most runners will generally do over the weekend).

Times over Short Distances

Fitness can also be judged by your performance in shorter distance races. If speed and anaerobic capacity are improving here, it is possible to predict a similar improvement or readiness for the longer distances, particularly for longer races like marathons (42km; 26 miles), which can be physically damaging and mentally tiring.

And so Bill Rodgers (USA) knew in 1975 that he was superfit and ready to run a world-class marathon: he had placed third over 12km (7.5 miles) in the World Cross Country Championships a few weeks beforehand. For a marathoner to do so well over 12km against the shorter-distance cross-country specialist was an exceptional performance. Rodgers knew he was ready and he was right: he set a US record for the 1975 Boston Marathon, winning in 2:09:55. In the same way, 10km (6-mile) runners can determine their own fitness by the relative speed they achieve over 1, 3 or 5km (½, 2 or 3 miles). It is not always necessary to race the target distance to gauge your fitness.

RIGHT *Psychological factors such as mental focus and positive mindplay perform a very important role in particularly long runs. This is when the moral support from friends during a training run or fellow club members during a race can get you through a difficult patch. Often, too, seasoned runners are able to share their own valuable experience.*

TECHNIQUES THAT WILL IMPROVE YOUR PERFORMANCE

Many runners determine their fitness from quality training sessions. Whether they run track intervals, fartlek (see p68), short distance or long distance races or hill repeats is not important; it is that the stopwatch records fast times for these sessions and the runners can determine how hard they worked to achieve such times. A good time is a fair indication of fitness; just as important is the apparent ease with which one did this.

Before his 1980 Olympic triumph in the 1500m heat, Sebastian Coe and his coach, father Peter Coe, knew that he was in shape for a gold medal because he was able to run six 800m (880yd) repetitions on the road in under two minutes with a very short rest in-between each repetition. A short rest with fast recovery is an indisputable sign of superfitness.

Injured before the 1984 Olympic trials in Los Angeles, USA, Steve Cram of Great Britain ran a specially organized 1500m speed trial at his home track in Gateshead. The world-class time he ran told him and his coaching team that he should make the trip to Los Angeles — which he did. Cram came in second after Sebastian Coe in an extremely fast time (Coe became the only man to defend an Olympic 1500m title).

LSD (Long Slow Distance running)

LSD is usually associated with mind-altering substances, particularly since the Beatles sang 'Lucy in the Sky with Diamonds', but for distance runners the term stands for Long Slow Distance. This forms the backbone of every distance runner's training regime. Long, paced runs play a significant role in any training programme; everything else is geared around this most important session and adds gloss to the basic product. And although LSD running is about testing yourself out in terms of distance, it should be undertaken at an easy, fun pace.

The great American 'fun' runner, Joe Henderson — also a long-time columnist at *Runner's World* (USA) — was the one to popularize LSD running. He set out to make running fun and he maintained that a thoroughly enjoyable tour of the suburbs and countryside at an easy relaxed pace would create lifetime runners — ones who would be committed to running regularly throughout every week of their lives. LSD still forms the basis for elite runners as well. They and their coaches understand that speed, speed-endurance and strength can be developed in alternative training sessions. LSD builds the foundation of great fitness, teaching the distance runner to become accustomed to the physical challenge of remaining vertical for many hours. This form of training can at the same time be put to creative use as the hours on the road free the brain to wander and to think through issues.

At one stage LSD running was very fashionable, and it was believed that it was possible to produce Olympic stars trained on long slow distance alone. We now know this to be fallacious and that LSD is one part, albeit an important part, of a complete training diet.

Long Fast Distance

The opposite of LSD, long fast distance is a potentially destructive training method. One or two longish runs at speed can help to develop pace but too many of these break down runners, resulting

LEFT *There are several spots on your wrist where you can take your pulse; what's most important is to feel a strong beat that will enable you to measure its frequency against the seconds of your watch.*

in injuries and sickness. Long, fast, distance running is more often than not undertaken by runners who need reassurance that they are ready to race a marathon. For instance, they will run 30–35km (15–20 miles) at a steady fast pace. Instead of relying on their shorter speed sessions to tell them what they wish to know, they run abreast at race pace for a route length that's close to their race distance. More often than not their best running is left behind on the training route rather than on the important race day.

It is really not necessary for runners to run hard over long distances to check that they are ready.

Speed Endurance

This session has elements of the long fast distance training run but is not ridiculously long. The run that is usually undertaken midweek or at the weekend is now run at a steady to fast pace over a distance shorter than your intended race distance but longer than any of the weekly runs. So, for instance, a runner intending to tackle a half marathon (21km; 13 miles) might set out on a speed endurance run of close to the intended half-marathon race pace but only for 7–10km (4–6 miles).

This session builds excellent speed endurance and also helps the runner to identify the correct pace for race day.

Interval Training

Interval training consists of repeated hard runs over a measured distance with recovery periods of easy, relaxed running or walking in-between. Interval training for elite runners can be very punishing. With hard repetitions being followed by very short rests, elite athletes may run five x 1.5km (1-mile) repeats, each in 4:45 with a one-leg 400m (440yd) jog recovery.

Intervals may be in ladder-form:

e.g. 400m > 600m > 800m > 1000m < 800m < 600m < 400m

or   440yd > 660yd > 880yd > 1100yd < 880yd < 660yd < 440yd

The basic aim is the same: to elevate the heart rate, cardiovascular and muscular systems and so on to close to maximum effort and then allow these to recover, before pushing yourself again. By pushing yourself to your limits, you train your body to cope with the resulting fatigue, or what is known as 'oxygen debt': with the added load on the muscles, they are unable to take in oxygen fast enough to burn fuel for energy. This method brings fantastic

RIGHT *Most seasoned runners will confirm that after having introduced regular bouts of interval training into their weekly schedule — on a track or along a measured stretch of road — they have improved their pace and as a result have run faster races.*

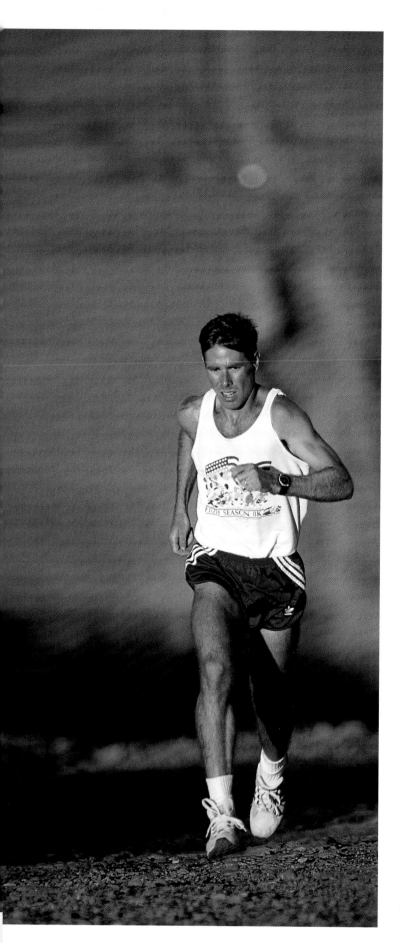

cardiovascular fitness and trains the legs and body to race under oxygen debt conditions. Elite athletes push their fitness to maximum by shortening their rest intervals as much as possible, though sessions need not be as gruelling for all runners. Run moderately and allow yourself plenty of recovery time; it is more important to keep the pace of your hard runs constant, so make sure you recover fully after each one. Shortening the rest intervals in-between will happen naturally over time as your fitness increases.

Understand, too, the importance of rest after such sessions, as overloading of the muscles causes microtears in the tendons and muscular system which need to be given time to recover. These could otherwise turn into more serious injuries.

Fartlek (Speedplay)

Linked to intervals is the less formal interval training method of fartlek, which is the Swedish word for 'speedplay'. Fartlek is less structured and can be run more for fun than as a serious speed-work session. It takes away the monotony of structured speedwork. Runners may jog across country, running fast from one tree to the next, then recovering from that tree to a distant stone wall. Or they may pace themselves between lampposts, running hard for four lampposts, then two easy, for part of the run. Fartlek is not a method of avoiding hard work but rather a way of making the whole experience as enjoyable as possible. Where a structured interval session allows fitness progress to be strictly monitored, fartlek allows this progress to be enjoyed.

Hillwork

Hillwork can be used, like interval training and fartlek, to increase cardiovascular fitness. It also promotes tremendous strength. Hillwork is rather like a weight workout session done at speed since you have to carry your body — against the pull of gravity — up a steep incline. It is harder work as the legs are not able to turn over as quickly as on flat terrain.

Running on the flat teaches you to do just that; it does not promote great hill climbing strength. So to do this, runners simply have to run hills. They can be run as quickly and as hard as desired, depending on the runner's intent. Try to incorporate them into as many of your training routes as possible as this keeps your hill running strength at an optimum. The shorter, steeper hills build strength and speed, while longer, gradual slopes build endurance. Any runner contemplating doing a race over a hilly course would be foolish not to train on some hills from time to time.

LEFT *In addition to the many strengthening benefits of hillwork, it also has the potential for less injury since the body is forced to slow down.*

Structured hill training sessions are also very useful and most top track and distance running athletes use this type of training to develop their speed, speed-endurance and strength. Bill Squires, legendary coach of the Boston Track Club in Massachusetts, USA, and advisor to Bill Rodgers (four-times Boston Marathon winner), has always been a big fan of hill training.

To get the benefit of a structured hill training session, runners should select a hill of between 400 and 600m (440 and 660yd) in length and having a steep gradient. After a 3—4km (2—2½-mile) warm-up, the hill should be run at a brisk effort. Bill Squires encourages runners to pull on an imaginary rope with loose but firm hands; the pulling movement coupled with good striding helps to launch the runner up the hill. It is important to concentrate on style and running form. Make an effort to maintain a good posture — take short strides, keeping your feet directly beneath your torso. By training yourself properly in the beginning, you will keep a good running form even when your body is tired, especially in a race. Try not to tire on the way up, so slowing down. This is why the hill should be no longer than 600m (660yd) — any longer and the striding part of the running required becomes a plod. The run back down to the base of the hill should be used for recovery. Downhills are also a good form of training, as the quadriceps (thigh muscles) undergo eccentric muscle contraction — the muscles lengthen under load (while bearing your body weight). Beginners should attempt to tackle the uphill five to six times.

Training on Sand Dunes

Sand dune running is really an extension of the hill running concept. Sand dunes are tougher of course, because the sand tugs and pulls at the ankle and the foot slides back with each upward stride. The benefits, though, are enormous as this increases a runner's strength. Many famous runners have used dune running to get fitter. Australian Herb Elliot (Olympic 1500m champion in 1960) ran up and down the sand dunes of Portsea, Australia; Briton Steve Ovett (Olympic 800m champion in 1980) used the legendary 'Big Dipper' on Merthyr Mawr in Wales; while South African Josia Thugwane (1996 Olympic Marathon champion) trained on the sand of Johannesburg's mine dumps to develop his strength.

Note: you could also try, as your level of fitness improves, to increase the length of time that you run each day by five minutes — but only do so in plateaus so that your body can adjust to the extra work it is required to do.

Beginner's training schedule		
Starting from scratch to running a 10km (6-mile) race in four months		
Monday		Rest day
Tuesday	5km / 3 miles	Run at your own pace
Wednesday	6km / 4 miles	Alternate briskly walking 1km (½ mile) with running 1km
Thursday		Rest day
Friday	5km / 3 miles	Run at your own pace
Saturday	5km / 3 miles	Alternate running between two or three lampposts with walking between the next two or three
Sunday	8km / 5 miles	Alternate running with walking, but try to complete this session eventually without walking.

CROSS-TRAINING

It is a well-known fact that the best training for running is running itself. However, there are benefits to be had from cross-training, particularly if a runner is injured. The greatest benefit is that the high-impact pounding is often avoided while the cardiovascular benefits are still retained. Cross-training is really only for those wanting to be the best. If time is limited, then run. If time is not a luxury, some benefit can be had by doing a measure of cross-training as outlined below.

Working out on a Treadmill

Running on a treadmill is one way of avoiding inclement weather. The great Norwegian distance runner, Ingrid Kristiansen, trained on a treadmill for hours during the height of the Scandinavian winter. This type of running is less impactful on the legs, however runners do have to be cautious. In the restricted indoor space of this machine, it is possible to take a nasty spill if you are not vigilant. Runners also have to drink often as the stationary running results in no air cooling, there is no wind chill factor, and runners can lose litres of fluid.

Nowadays the sophistication of treadmills allows you to programme for undulating courses or a measured series of interval workouts. Treadmill running does tend to be very boring, though, with none of the terrain or scenery changes of the outdoors. In fact, what it does do is serve as a reminder of how sociable and enjoyable road running is!

Swimming and Running in Water

Runners do not usually make good swimmers and vice versa — which is what makes the leading triathletes such outstanding performers. They are able to combine two sports which in many ways are mutually exclusive. However swimming is a great way of keeping fit, particularly when suffering any injuries. Some runners will also train by running in the shallow end of a pool; this generates tremendous resistance with minimal impact. It may be boring and difficult but running through water is certainly one way of keeping the endorphins flowing and ensuring that you get your exercise.

Cold water has wonderful restorative powers for tired, swollen legs and it is no coincidence that trainers and breeders like to canter their race horses on the edge of the sea to help them recover after a hard gallop. We can't all have access to the sea but those who do can benefit enormously from short runs or walks in ankle-deep, cold seawater.

Cycling

Cycling is a valuable cross-training sport for runners. The legs, lungs and head are exercised, pushing up blood circulation but without the pounding of the muscles. Many runners like to cycle to and from training venues to warm up the legs and to aid recovery. A long weekend run can cause quite a bit of leg pain and stiffness, and cycling the same evening helps to relieve the muscular aches. An easy course without major hills should be selected, requiring an easy (high) gear. The idea is to spin gently for a while without the need for any heavy (low) gears. Certainly many triathletes and duathletes have noticed tremendous benefits from combining running with cycling.

Note, that there are two categories of cyclists: those who have crashed and those who are soon to crash. Cycling may be a low-impact sport, but it isn't when you fall off! Exercise extreme caution when cycling and always wear a helmet.

Walking

Walking is a useful aid to running, particularly for distance runners busy starting their running career (both beginners and experienced). Beginners often need to walk during early training sessions and should incorporate walking breaks into these. Even well-seasoned runners also advocate walking breaks during the running of a marathon or ultramarathon (many an experienced marathoner has had no choice but to walk after 'hitting the wall' [see p78] during such a race).

Gymwork

Weight- and gymwork can be very time-consuming so once again, runners should remember that the best training for running is running. But for those runners who have the luxury of time, working out in the gym and lifting weights can help to enhance strength and resistance to the pounding that runners tend to sustain. For marathons that incorporate long punishing downhills in their routes, weightwork can help to control the damaging effects of such courses.

After having experienced a gruelling Comrades (South Africa) race on the 'down' course in 1982, I consulted sports scientist Tim Noakes who worked out a schedule of weightwork for me to follow to strengthen my calves as well as my shoulders and chest area. These sessions helped enormously, particularly in later 'down' races.

FAR LEFT AND CENTRE *Cycling, swimming and snow-shoeing all promote an excellent cardiovascular workout, expanding the lungs and strengthening the chest cavity. Snow-shoeing works, too, on the leg muscles while swimming is known for its all-round benefits to the arms, shoulders, back and legs. Cycling also works on strengthening the legs but, most importantly, without the jarring stress on the bones.*

LEFT *Running knee-deep through water provides an added resistance to the lower legs for a stronger workout, while icy seawater promotes the contraction of swollen veins.*

STRETCHING

When we exercise, we put our muscles through a constant contraction-relaxation process since one set of muscles has to relax, or lengthen, in order to allow an opposing set to contract. With running we are continually using the same sets of leg muscles, which are being made to contract repeatedly. If they are not regularly stretched, they learn to adjust to these shorter lengths and the result is tight, short muscles that are increasingly resistant to lengthening.

When we experience tightness in our muscles, it is because they are being exercised through a partial, rather than their full, range of motion. Stiff muscles inhibit the flexibility of the joints, thus impeding the flow of lubricating fluids. In not lengthening fully, they prevent the opposing muscles from contracting to their fullest extent, and so lose strength and tone; they also cause misalignment of the body through the imbalance of opposing muscle groups.

Although there are arguments against stretching by those who claim to have suffered injuries from it, there is enough evidence to support the fact that if stretching exercises are done properly, they can improve muscle elasticity, flexibility and strength — in joints and connective tissue as well as the muscle itself. The risk of injury is lessened because the muscles are more resilient, and as a result are able to stretch through a greater range of motion.

The best form of stretch is known as static stretching; the opposite of this is dynamic stretching, which is jerky because one bounces into position. The stretch is held very briefly, a few seconds at most. Rather, a runner should ease into each stretch slowly and gently till he or she feels a tightness (but *no* pain) in the muscle being stretched, and hold that position for at least 30 seconds — up to a minute if possible.

Going into it gradually prevents the stimulation of a mechanism in the muscles which protects them from being overstretched. When a muscle is lengthened, tiny receptors attached to the muscle fibres sense this and send a message to the nerves that control muscle contraction. At the point that the muscle is being overstretched, stronger warning signals are sent by the receptors and the muscle instinctively contracts.

Runners will notice that after holding a stretch for 30 seconds or so, they can push it a little further without experiencing any pain, and continue to do this at regular intervals. There is a feeling that the muscle 'gives' at a certain point. What occurs is called 'inverse stretch reflex'; in this case, receptors in the tendons work to *prevent* the muscle from contracting thus protecting the tendons from tearing. The 'give' is the relaxation of all the remaining tension in the muscle.

Recommended stretch exercises

Most runners will want to limber up half an hour to 15 minutes before starting a race, so the usefulness of many of the following stretches is that thay can be done in the outdoors, with the aid of low walls, embankments, concrete posts, trees and so on. They cover the most important running muscle groups.

Hold the pose for at least 30 seconds and repeat each exercise two or three times for each leg.

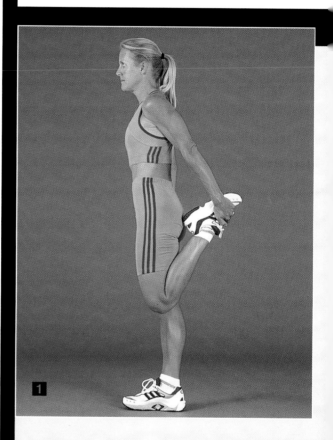

1 Quadriceps

With your right hand, balance yourself against a wall or tree while using the left hand to grasp your left ankle. Pull the heel of the lower bent leg straight back (not to the side) toward your buttock to stretch the quadriceps of the front thigh, keeping your back as straight as possible. Those who have good balance control can do this without steadying themselves. Repeat for the right leg.

CALF STRETCHES

2 Calf muscles

Tilt your foot up against a stair, kerb, post or tree with your heel placed firmly on the ground and lean forward, straight-backed, to stretch the calf muscle. Alternate your feet.

3 Lower calf/Achilles tendon

Leaning against a wall or tree with straight (or bent arms, depending on your height and the flexibility of your muscles), step forward with one leg (keeping it bent) and stretch the other straight, as far behind you as you can. You should feel the Achilles tendon and lower calf muscle lengthening. Make sure you tilt the hips forward but keep the back straight. Also, firmly push down the back of the heel of the outstretched leg to intensify the stretch. Then alternate with the other leg.

4 Alternative calf stretch

Instead of stretching the second leg straight behind you, bend it almost to the same degree that you're holding your first leg, and hold this position. You should feel the stretch in your calf, or soleus, muscle. Alternate.

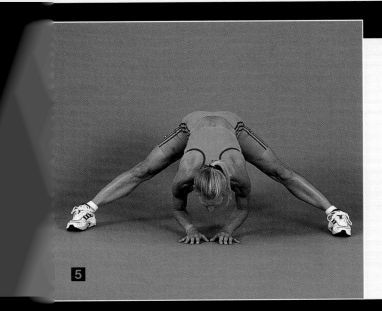

5 Extended leg stretch

This stretch borrowed from Yoga is excellent for a simultaneous lengthening of the adductor, hamstring and calf muscles. Spread feet as far apart as possible and lean forward from the waist. Place your hands, arms bent, on the ground as close to the centre (directly beneath you) as possible and hold. Those who are more supple will eventually be able to rest their head lightly on the ground between their hands. To come out of this pose, keep a straight back and slowly raise your torso with your hands on your hips before working your feet inward to be able to step them together.

1

2 side

2 frontal

HAMSTRINGS

1 Horizontal stretch on a chair or low wall

If you're outdoors, stretch out one leg on a low wall otherwise substitute a chair for indoors. Do not lift the leg to a ninety-degree angle to your body; this is too high and could overstretch your muscles. Keep the foot flexed but ankles relaxed. Maintaining a straight back, lean forward from the waist with arms outstretched toward the toes and gently stretch the hamstring.

2 Vertical crossed-calf stretch

Standing upright, cross your legs at the ankles and bend forward at the waist, keeping your head relaxed and hanging down. Grab your ankles or touch the ground with your fingers as best you can to feel the stretch in your hamstrings. You will find that after holding this pose for 30 seconds, you can push yourself lower and get your forehead closer to your knees (the tension relaxes in your muscles, which allows you to lengthen them further).

Re-cross your ankles and repeat to emphasize the stretch in the other leg.

Bent-knee sit-ups

Lie on your back with your knees bent and your feet on the floor. Clasp your hands behind the head and raise yourself to a sitting position, then slowly lower yourself back to the floor again. Do a set of 20, rest, then repeat for 20. This strengthens the abdominal muscles.

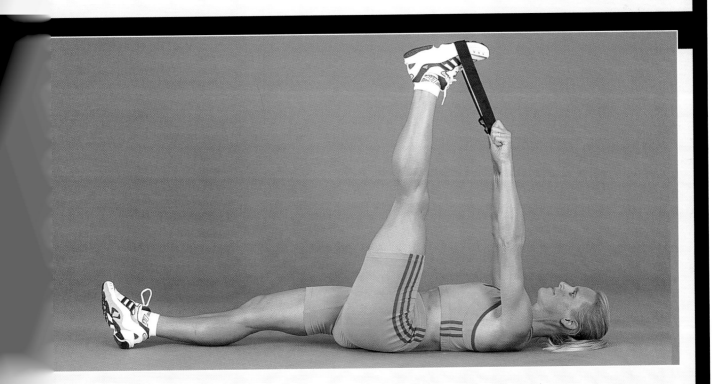

Hamstring stretch

This is another stretch borrowed from Yoga. Lie on the floor with one leg outstretched, and loop a rope or belt around the inner heel of the other leg, pulling the rope taut and using it to slowly straighten the leg to a ninety-degree angle with the torso. Straighten the raised leg as much as possible, pulling it toward you with the belt. This is an excellent stretch for the Achilles tendon, calf, hamstring and gluteal (buttock) muscles. Alternate legs.

Note that no specific weights have been recommended here as these will obviously vary depending on a runner's size and strength. You will need to judge your own level of fitness.

CALVES

▌1▐ Calf raises

Set the weights, rest the pads on your shoulders and step on the platform. Raise yourself on the balls of your feet and hold before slowly lowering your heels. Do two to three sets of 10.

QUADRICEPS, HIPS AND HAMSTRINGS

▌2▐ Half-squats with bar-bell

This exercise strengthens the hips, the quadricep muscles of the thighs and the hamstrings.

With the feet spaced hip-width apart and angled slightly outwards, balance a suitably weighted bar-bell comfortably on your shoulders, gripping the bar from behind with both hands. Making sure to keep the back straight, bend the knees and lower your body to a partial squat position, slowly straightening up again. Do this 15 to 25 times, depending on your personal strength and fitness.

▌3▐ Lunge with bar-bell

This exercise focuses on the quadriceps. Using the same weighted bar-bell as for the half-squats, balance it on your shoulders and grip as above. Step forward into a half-lunge, keeping the back straight, then slowly straighten up.

Do this 20 times, then alternate legs and repeat.

▌4▐ Bench steps with bar-bell

This exercise will strengthen the hips and thighs. Balance the bar-bell on your shoulders, again gripping it from behind with both hands, then step up and down on a low one- or two-stepped bench 15 to 25 times.

Change legs and repeat session.

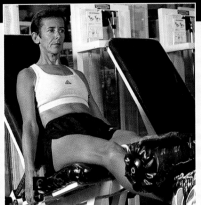

HAMSTRINGS AND QUADRICEPS

5 Hamstring curls

This strengthens the hamstrings. Lying flat on the leg extension bench, grip the handles with your hands and hook your heels under the padded roller. Bend the lower legs, raising the roller toward your buttocks before slowly lowering it to its original position. Do three sets of 15.

6 Leg extensions

These exercises will strengthen the quadriceps. Seated on the leg extension chair, hook your feet under the padded roller and lift it as high to the horizontal as possible, slowly lowering it to its original position. Do this 20 times. Increase number of repetitions rather than weight.

CHEST AND SHOULDERS

7 Dumbbell pullovers

Strengthens and opens up the rib cage, improving lung capacity. Holding a dumbbell in each hand, lie on a bench and straighten out the arms behind your head, while inhaling deeply, till arms are parallel to the floor. Exhale while raising the arms to a ninety-degree angle above the chest (it is important to breathe correctly). Repeat 10 times.

8 Lateral supine raises

Strengthens the chest and shoulder muscles. Again, breathing is important. Holding a dumbbell in each hand, lie on a bench this time with the arms bent out sideways. Exhale as you raise the arms vertically above your chest, then inhale as you bend and lower the arms outwards (your chest expands at the same time). Do this 10 times.

ADAPTING YOUR RUNNING SCHEDULE INTO FAMILY LIFE

Although running is one of the quickest, easiest and most time-efficient of sports, requiring very little preparation (running gear on, shoes on and out the door; no courts to be booked, no playing partner picked up), it nevertheless does take time out of the daily regime of family and work life. So whether it is done from home, from the office, in a foreign city, and at different times of the day, it does need to be carefully structured if there is a chance that it is going to impact on family or work associates.

For these reasons, most runners like to run early in the morning. As hard as it is, the routine of getting up with the alarm to go out running can quite quickly become just that, part of your routine. But the popular approach seems to be an early morning run, a quick shower, breakfast and then to work or to spend time with the family. With the run done, the rest of the day is free for other commitments.

Of course, there are disadvantages, especially in winter when it is cold and dark, and it can be very tough to drag a warm, weary body out into the elements. Early morning running can also result in 'early afternoon dozing'. The 'graveyard' time just after lunch takes on a fresh meaning for first-time runners. Generally, though, it is an extremely satisfying way to start the day, with the endorphins that have been stimulated by the exercise making you feel energized.

RIGHT *An apt term that correctly encapsulates the experience, 'hitting the wall' is something that myriad runners have had the misfortune to encounter. However, experts will tell you that taking care to restore your depleted glycogen levels during the race by ingesting carbohydrates will keep that dreaded wall at bay.*

Hitting the wall

This describes the physical experience usually felt at the 32km (20-mile) marker of a standard marathon (42.4km; 26.2 miles) by runners who have judged their pace incorrectly and started too quickly. The feeling descends on the runner so swiftly that the sudden switch from running strongly and fast to running through what feels like thick mud with a dizzy head and weak limbs is like hitting a brick wall. Experienced runners avoid the wall by running within their own 'red line' limits (From Half to Ultramarathon, p122) and by taking extra carbohydrates and fighting off dehydration. Any runner who hits the wall will not want to experience it again.

Blow

This phrase also means to hit the wall, or tire drastically in a race. The 'blow' here could be the puffing, panting noise a runner makes when exhausted, blowing like a surfacing whale; the allusion could also be to 'blow up', as in an explosion.

Second half of the race

A seemingly obvious phrase that in running terminology is not so obvious. 'The second half' is that part of the race that doesn't match the actual distance in length but is so tough and gruelling that it appears to take as long as the first half of the race. The 'second half' of a 42km (26-mile) marathon begins at 30km (18 miles), the second half of a 21km (13-mile) half marathon from 15km (9 miles). The second half of an ultramarathon of 100km (62 miles) is somewhere between 75 and 80km (46 and 50 miles). The idea is to reach this 'second half' feeling as strong as possible.

A bus

A 'bus' is a term given to a group of runners who are running together in a race (or during a runner's club training run) at a similar pace with a common finishing time in mind. Shared discipline is easier than individual discipline (which is hard work) so a bus runs as a group and shares the workload. Members of the bus can shelter behind each other in winds, they can consult on pace judgement and they can share drinks at refreshment and seconding tables. They can also encourage each other. At the start of a race, runners may even seek out a bus with which to run. This can be a four-hour marathon bus or a one-hour 10km (6-mile) one; each has a similar end objective.

Buses can have bus 'drivers' — one or two experienced runners who guide the bus and who judge pace and effort. Drivers can steer or drive the bus from the back or front of the group; they often split the responsibility with one driver in front and one behind the bus.

Carbo-loading

This is the now popularized procedure of loading the muscles and liver with glycogen or fuel for a long distance run. For two or three days before a race, runners will emphasize the carbohydrates in their meals, particularly complex carbohydrates, in order to develop a full 'fuel tank' for race day. So, complex carbohydrates such as rice, bread, bananas and pasta are eaten to boost carbohydrate stores. We now know that the body burns glycogen from carbohydrates when exercising, and the old idea of steak and eggs before battle is incorrect. Carbo-loading is essential when racing beyond 32km (20 miles).

Splits

'Splits' are time gaps between competing runners or times taken at significant distance markers along a race route e.g. the split between Rosa Mota of Portugal and Belgium's Agnes Pardaens at the end of the 1987 Boston Marathon was 4:30; in winning in 2:25:21 Mota was 4½ minutes ahead of Pardaens. In the same race, the men's split for the half-marathon distance marker was 1:06:22, i.e. the lead pack including eventual winner Toshihiko Seko of Japan went through the halfway point in one hour, six minutes and 22 seconds. By international standards, this was not a fast split at all.

Bailing

Rather like bailing out of an aeroplane, this means to drop out of a race — not desired, but sometimes unavoidable. Bailing is the same as DNF (below).

DNF

Did Not Finish — bailed — no more need be said.

DNS

Did Not Start — for any variety of reasons.

Seconds/pacers

Generally frowned upon today, seconds and pacers were more common in the past when they brought information, drinks, and a change of shoes to their runners. They are now more often seen in ultramarathons where the physical challenge of the race demands extra care and attention. The ultimate pacing or seconding job is probably at the Western States 100 Miler in the USA where pacers can end up running/walking up to 40 miles [64km] with their runners' equipment. This includes trudging up and down steep valleys, at times through snow or in 90°F. (32°C) heat, and fording a number of streams. Pacers/seconds are often subject to a lot of abuse from their runners ('I said I wanted water, not that junk! Go back and get me what I requested!'). Pacers may also be vomited on, they have to treat and dress blisters, and goad and bully their runner to the finish line. Think carefully before volunteering!

PB

Personal Best — a runner's personal record of the best time that he or she has achieved over a specific distance, either in a training run or in a race.

Aid station/watering table

Refreshment and first-aid tables situated at strategic spots along a race route.

Other runners prefer to run during their lunch hour, claiming that it is more fun at midday, that the legs are loose and warmed up by then — and that this allows them to sleep in the morning! In addition, running works as a natural appetite suppressor for a few hours, so, if you are planning to lose weight, what better time to run than at lunchtime? Running can take the place of eating. The disadvantage is that in the workplace, access to shower facilities is not always possible, and running gear has to be packed for each day. In the summer in hotter countries, lunchtime running can be very draining too because of the heat and humidity.

Many runners train at night or in the evenings when the day's activities are over. This can be very pleasant, especially in the cool of evening. The disadvantages here are that it is easy to be distracted and to end up not going through with these sessions. When arriving home tired or irritable it is very tempting to sink into a comfortable chair and never emerge!

Experienced or hardened runners will tend to vary their running times to take the monotony out of running and will allow for the different structure of each day. So, on some days they will run in the early morning, on others they will run at night, and yet others at midday. They have learnt to be flexible at all times, which is the key to successful running and to keeping work colleagues, family and friends happy.

Running can take on different priorities at different times. When a big race for you personally is approaching, you can ask the family for their sympathy and understanding. Once the race is over, the running can take second place to other demands. If you always keep others informed of your running plans, they will usually be helpful and sympathetic.

The family, too, needs to make allowances for the stress and strain of training for a major race. Long distance races, particularly marathons, are tiring physically and as race day approaches, can be nerve-wracking psychologically. Distance runners who are normally extremely tolerant people can become irritable, short-tempered, even so far as resembling prima donnas in their behaviour! The family needs to understand this in advance and make allowances. The runner must then show his or her gratitude afterwards by rewarding the family and making running a lesser priority. Happily the recovery process makes this fairly easy to do. But before race day, Saturday nights may have to be boring and early-to-bed nights; after race day, there is no reason why they should.

ENTERING YOUR FIRST RACE

Inevitably most runners have the desire to race — whether it is against themselves, the stopwatch or other runners. We are competitive animals and we like to see how we compare with others. Races can be very intimidating, however, and it is best to start small and grow from there. For your first race, choose a short distance run, preferably a local fun run (of between 5 and 10km, or 3 and 6 miles) that does not cost too much in time or money. If you join a running club, you can learn about the race calendar for your area from them; otherwise, the Internet is a good source for annual road running schedules.

Plan the race well in advance and enter well before, although many races do only accept entries on race day. Make sure you know where to enter, where to park your car, and the race start and finish points. On the day itself, allow time for packing your running paraphernalia, the travel there, and entry procedures at the race location (which involves paying a fee and receiving a number or a small entry card which you pin to your shorts for the race).

LEFT *Running is an activity that can be participated in by the entire family, young and old. It should be impressed upon the younger members, though, that they will need to take care to pursue their training slowly — and in plateaus — so that their softer and more flexible, still-developing bone structure can adjust to the additional stresses that are being placed on it.*

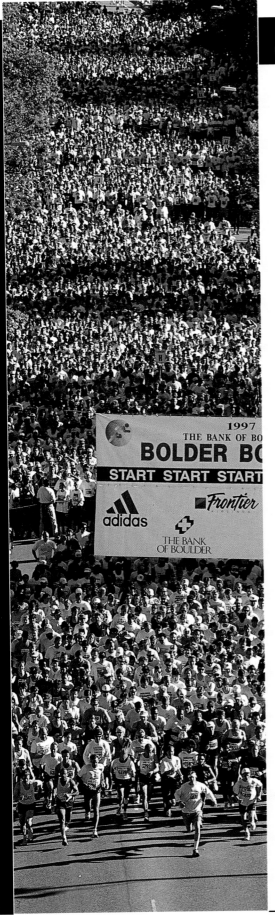

Preparing for your first race

The following pointers will help you prepare yourself for your first race:

▶ Enter with a friend of equal fitness; the shared experience is a lot more fun and you will have a running companion for the entire route.

▶ Make sure that none of your clothing — especially socks and shoes — is new, but has been fully worn-in on several of the longer training runs.

▶ Line up at the start with runners of similar abilities. It is tempting to line up near the front in order to achieve the best possible time but it can also be enormously offputting. Being swept into a pace that is too fast and too exhausting is a tough experience, and you will get pushed and shoved out of the way by the faster runners. Start at a reasonable pace for your own ability and work your way through the field in your own time.

▶ Always start slowly, and rather finish running strongly than in a state of collapse because you used up all your energy reserves trying to keep up with faster runners. There is so much to learn about racing that you can improve later, in further races. Try instead to enjoy the experience.

▶ Take advantage of the aid stations/watering tables manned by volunteers, which may offer water, Coca-Cola, or locally branded sports drinks at various intervals in the race. Keep yourself well hydrated; the drinks are a good source of sugar to boost your energy. Aid stations are strictly controlled in international championships. During a major marathon, they may also carry stocks of Vaseline, plasters (Band-Aid), chocolate, and even massage ointments and masseurs. Ambulances (ominously) may also be parked at these stations.

▶ Don't be disheartened by the number of people passing you during the race. There will always be runners way ahead of you — and also behind you!

▶ It may be useful to carry your own energy-boosting supplements, available at any sports store, such as mini-sachets of glucose syrup or glucose/fructose tablets in your shorts pocket.

▶ Find out beforehand what the cut-off time for the race is, so that you can correctly pace yourself for it. Although the time is displayed in electronic panels at the race finish, wear your own running watch so you can monitor your progress during the event. For a 10km (6-mile) race, a cutoff time of 1½ hours is usually allowed; for 15km (9 miles), from 1:40 to 2:00 (depending on the degree of difficulty).

▶ For the longer race, it is useful to fold sheets of tissue or toilet paper into a small transparent bank bag to pin to the inside of your shorts, in the event of an emergency pit-stop. (It is very common for race nerves to unsettle a runner's stomach.)

Nutrition
and diet

A LONG-DISTANCE RUNNER MORE THAN ANY OTHER SPORTSPERSON NEEDS TO FOCUS ON CORRECT EATING HABITS.

A BALANCED EATING PLAN

Running is a hard, draining sport and it is important for marathoners to be aware of correct nutrition at all times. In being (generally) very driven, committed people, runners unfortunately can be convinced at times to try extraordinary diet plans in order to gain a winning edge or to lose those few kilograms.

One problem is that running is very dependent on strength-to-weight ratio. There are many examples of runners who have become too extreme in an attempt to lose as much weight as possible and this ends up being detrimental to their health. It is also no coincidence that running — with its emphasis on discipline and control — tends to attract the anorexic personality.

First of all it is important to emphasize that runners generally experience tremendous health benefits because of their running. For those who are badly overweight when they start running, a balanced, controlled diet combined with exercise can play an enormously beneficial role in helping with weight loss. (An overweight runner who starts by running too frequently, too fast and too hard can suffer back, knee and ankle injuries because the skeleton, tendons and ligaments are placed under considerable stress by the impact of the overweight body.) A sensible diet that is combined with moderate exercise to start off with can lead to the desired weight loss without the accompanying danger.

It is also important for those runners who believe that running is the panacea for all evils — and gives them carte blanche to eat whatever they like — to realize it is not. Even the slimmest and fittest of runners need to understand the dangers of cholesterol, junk food and chemical additives.

The key for a successful marathon runner is balance, common sense and restraint. It is important for runners to follow a balanced diet with as much protein, carbohydrate and fat as is necessary to fuel their particular workload. They also need to understand the role vitamins and mineral supplements can play and to incorporate a daily regime of these supplements in order to give the exercising body every advantage.

Over the years there have been a number of fad diets linked to sport. Some have stayed (e.g. the carbohydrate-loading regimen) but most have faded or are no longer fashionable. In years to come there will no doubt be other crazes. In the end, however, good distance running appears to go hand-in-glove with sensible, clear-headed eating patterns.

LEFT AND RIGHT *Runners such as famous international athlete Uta Pippig of Germany (left) — winner of two Boston Marathons — learn early on in their running career to be aware of correct nutrition. Suddenly stepping up one's training programme leads to a natural increase in appetite as the body's cravings indicate its need for additional fuel to replenish the energy reserves that are being used up during the increased activity.*

LISTEN TO THE BODY'S MESSAGES

It is amazing how the working body can tell runners what it requires. When placed under stress — for example, towards the end of a marathon — the body is designed to warn and guide you in terms of potential problems. Runners who have ever become hypoglycaemic (rapidly falling blood glucose levels) in a race know how awful the feeling is. One feels weak, drained, almost faint. The lips buzz and the fingertips tingle. The brain tends to feel as if it is stuffed with cloth rags rather than brain cells. The body is screaming for 'sugar, sugar, sugar' and its response after being fed sweets (candy), a carbohydrate-heavy meal, commercial soft drinks or patented sports drinks — can be instantaneous. One's running performance — or recovery, in this case — is instantly enhanced as long as carbohydrates are consumed. Runners at the end of a gruelling ultramarathon have often noted how the bruised and damaged muscles in their legs will send strong, powerful signals to their brain for a hefty steak with chips. The body is craving vital protein to repair the damage inflicted by the run.

Some runners have been known to crave salt, sweetened drinks or even ice cream. The significance is, in most cases, that the craving reflects the nutrient deficiency runners may be experiencing.

A well-known marathoner in the famous annual London to Brighton race was nicknamed Trevor 'Eat Soup' Parry because he craved dehydrated 'instant' soup towards the end of his race. His poor seconds had to run from shop to shop to buy a packet of powdered mushroom soup in order to sat-

isfy Parry's craving for what was probably salt or the sodium from MSG (monosodium glutamate).

Distance runners should learn to listen to these cravings, particularly when racing or training very hard.

THE BODY'S NUTRITIONAL NEEDS

Three food groups are essential in providing the body with energy thus enabling it to function properly: carbohydrates, proteins and fats. Next in vital importance are the vitamins, minerals and trace elements that exploit the energy created. For distance runners, however, carbohydrates are the single most important source of energy. Sports nutritionists are generally in agreement that, proportionally, an athlete's diet should consist of not less than 60 per cent carbohydrates, 15 per cent protein and at the most, 25 per cent fat. Certainly, the old idea that soldiers, football players and astronauts went into battle fuelled by steak and eggs is incorrect and outdated.

CARBOHYDRATES: THE RUNNER'S FUEL

Carbohydrates are the 'new' food for long distance. Once digested into glucose, they are stored in the liver and muscle cells in the form of glycogen and released into the bloodstream as the energy is required via the chemical process in which ATP (adenosine triphosphate) is broken down to ADP (adenosine diphosphate) and phosphate, releasing energy (see p25).

Carbohydrates consist of both simple and complex carbohydrates, the complex variety being best for a steady continuous supply of easily utilized energy. The simpler carbohydrates offer instant energy but this can cause surges in insulin and glycogen levels. The sudden boost to blood sugar levels stimulates the production of insulin, which then speeds up the conversion of glucose to glycogen in the muscle cells. The result is

LEFT *Because proteins help repair damaged muscle and tissue, some runners will find that they most crave a juicy steak (top) after a tough long-distance race. And one need feel no guilt eating chocolate (bottom) after exercise as the sugars will help restock the body's lowered glycogen levels.*

an instant drop in blood sugar levels, leaving the sportsperson feeling weak.

It is also possible to store carbohydrates in the liver by drinking fruit juices, sports drinks (which contain sugars), sweetened tea and coffee, and even sugared commercial soft drinks. The distance runner's body becomes very adept at storing carbohydrates (glycogen) as running involves a continual depleting and restocking of liver and muscle supplies. Any hard-training runner who cuts back on carbohydrate intake while increasing protein and fat intake will experience a decrease in energy levels after some time.

RIGHT *Carbohydrates raise blood sugar levels at differing rates (known as the glycaemic index). Honey, a simple carbohydrate, causes a faster rise in blood sugar (high glycaemic index) whereas more complex carbohydrates such as bananas, pasta or wholewheat bread cause a more sustained rise (low glycaemic index).*

Sources of carbohydrates

COMPLEX CARBOHYDRATES	SIMPLE CARBOHYDRATES
Potatoes	White bread
Rice	Sugar
Wholewheat products (pasta, bread)	Honey
Wholegrains (corn, oats, rye, barley)	Treacle
Maizemeal	Sweets (candy)
Bananas	Alcohol
Fresh and stewed fruit	

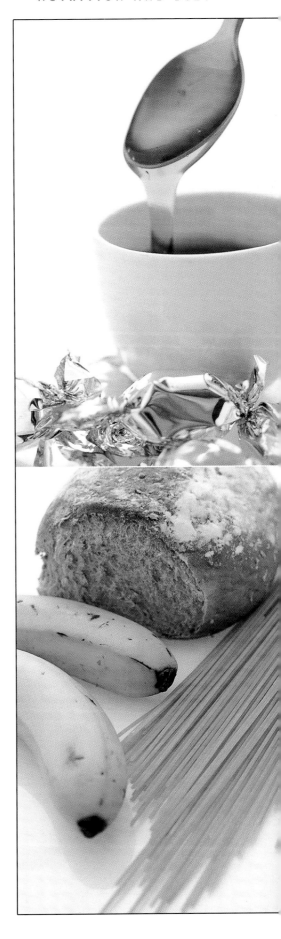

Carbohydrate-loading

Distance runners today are so convinced about the power of carbohydrates that if they are planning to race beyond 30km (18½ miles), they will carbo-load. This means storing as much energy and fuel in the muscles as possible two to three days before a marathon. It does not mean 'pigging out', but at each meal the marathoner should take in 90 per cent carbohydrates with only a little fat and protein consumed.

The most efficient way to take in and store this fuel is to concentrate on eating carbohydrates during the three-day loading period immediately before the race. Runners can also load their carbohydrate intake with simple candy (boiled sweets or peppermints) and a carbo-fortified sports drink.

Because the body is only able to convert glucose to glycogen at a certain rate, it is better to eat a number of smaller meals throughout the day than three large ones. If the body is bombarded with glucose, it will convert a given amount to glycogen and store the balance as fat.

Carbo-loading is also successfully achieved by ingesting specially formulated sports and energy drinks. For more detail on these, refer to p130 of the chapter From Half to Ultramarathon.

BELOW *A bowl of high-fibre cereal for breakfast, a filled baked potato at lunch (or dinner) and pasta in the evening illustrates an excellent daily regimen containing complex carbohydrates for the hard-working athlete.*

The Saltin Depletion Diet

This diet, invented by a Swedish physiologist, was originally used by cyclists. It involves a strict carbohydrate depletion period for three days after a final but hard workout to drain the muscles of glycogen. This is commenced six days before the final competition. The

A typical day of carbo-loading should include three meals	
Breakfast	Oat porridge with sugar and a dash of milk; toast, honey and jam; sweet tea or coffee; option of a carbo-loading sports drink.
Lunch	Pasta with a simple tomato sauce (cream-based sauces contain too much fat and can upset the stomach during the run); fruit such as bananas or raisins for dessert.
Supper	Potato in its jacket with a cheese filling or rice with a simple meat sauce; avocado salad; rice pudding or dried fruit.

three days before the event the athlete switches to a very high carbohydrate diet and the body then supposedly reacts by absorbing a superload of carbohydrates in response to the depletion phase. I have personally tried out the Saltin diet and love it, as does the great British runner Ron Hill, who used it successfully for his winning marathons in 1969, 1970 and 1971. Hill was a very big fan. However, there are many runners who hate the diet, and it has fallen out of favour.

Post-race Carbohydrate Replacement

Carbohydrate replacement after racing is very important in aiding recovery. Only about 500g (8oz) of glycogen can be stored in the muscle at any time, and these stocks are depleted during a race and prolonged or intensive training. If the glycogen levels are not restored, runners will feel a sluggishness in their legs on their next training run. Do bear in mind that in terms of energy spent, a fast-paced 10km (6-mile) run will burn up more carbohydrates than a leisurely paced 25km (16-mile) run.

A carbohydrate-enriched drink should be drunk as soon as possible after finishing a race (at least within the first two hours); this means 250ml (½pt) for a carbo-drink and 800—1000ml (1—2pt) for an energy sports drink. Thereafter a carbohydrate-weighted meal should be eaten. Instant high-carbohydrate snacks include three medium-sized fruits (apples, apricots, peaches) or a packet of low-fat pretzels. Scientific studies have shown that those distance runners who delay this replacement process recover far slower than those who are quick to consume carbohydrates.

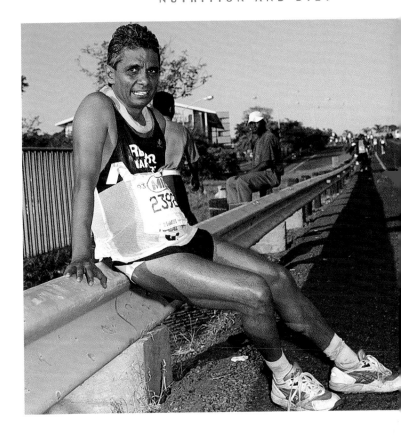

ABOVE *If, after an intensive run, you make no effort to replenish your body's glycogen levels by eating high-carbohydrate foods, you will experience a drained, 'dead-legged' feeling in your legs from the lack of fuel in your muscles that is necessary for renewed exercise.*

FATS

Fat is a highly concentrated energy source and provides far more energy than carbohydrates; as the exercising body becomes depleted of its glycogen energy sources, it gradually switches to metabolizing fat as an alternate source of fuel. Although a moderate amount of fat is essential to any diet, it is also important to be aware of the health dangers of consuming too much.

Saturated fats   Fats are either saturated and solid at room temperature, or unsaturated and liquid at room temperature, for example, vegetable oils. In terms of chemical composition, most fats occur as triglycerides. In saturated fats, most of the triglyceride molecule's chemical bonds are formed by hydrogen while unsaturated fats contain fewer hydrogen bonds. Animal fats as well as cocoa butter and coconut and palm oil are all saturated and have a tendency to raise LDL (low-density lipoprotein) levels, that is, increase the 'bad' cholesterol (see p19).

Polyunsaturated fats   These consist of omega-6 and omega-3 fatty acids. Omega-6 fats exist in most cooking oils, such as sunflower,

Sources of Fats

SATURATED			MONOUNSATURATED	POLYUNSATURATED
MEAT	DAIRY	VEGETABLE	VEGETABLE	VEGETABLE
Chicken skin	Full-cream milk	Vegetable oils	Olive oil	Flaxseed
Lard	Butter	Palm	Avocados	Corn
Suet	Cheese	Coconut	Nuts	Safflower
	Egg yolk	Cocoa butter		Sunflower
	Mayonnaise			Soyabean

PROTEIN

Although protein is a minor and unimportant fuel as far as exercise physiology is concerned (at best, it supplies 10 per cent of the body's energy requirements), it plays a crucial role in the body. Proteins contain nitrogen, which is essential to the formation — and maintenance — of the basic structure of body tissue; our hair, skin, muscles and blood cells all consist of protein, as do our hormones, enzymes and antibodies.

Most important to the athlete, protein is responsible for repairing damaged tissue and building stronger, more efficient muscles. Training undoubtedly increases the body's demand for protein and after long races this demand escalates. In recent years there has been some evidence that eating more protein prior to the ultra-long distance events may help to negate some of the muscle damage that could result.

LEFT *The nutrients provided by each of these foods are important to the working body for different reasons (from left to right): milk and cheese contain fats, proteins and calcium; specially fortified sports drinks offer athletes carbohydrates in addition to supplementary vitamins and electrolytes; and various types of meat provide protein — the building block of muscle.*

canola (rape seed), corn and safflower, and act by lowering blood cholesterol. Evening primrose oil also contains omega-6 fatty acids.

Omega-3 fats exist in oily fish such as salmon, mackerel, tuna, trout, herring, anchovies, and sardines — as well as in flaxseed (linseed) oil, wholegrains, soya beans, spinach and walnuts. These lower the number of triglycerides in the bloodstream (high levels are linked to high blood cholesterol) and, in thinning the consistency of blood, reduce the formation of blood clots.

Monounsaturated fats   Occurring in olive oil, avocados and nuts, these fatty acids lower LDL levels and possibly raise HDL (high-density lipoprotein) levels — the 'good' cholesterol which carries fat deposits from artery to liver to be excreted.

Fats are good for endurance running. Although more oxygen is used in the burning of fat than carbohydrates — so the energy comes with less oxygen available to the body — the energy provided is higher than that produced by an equal amount of carbohydrates. The fats are stored in the body's fat cells, where they exist 'muscle-bound' (or, in scientific terms, as intramuscular triglycerides) in the muscle fibres.

It is believed that in particularly long-distance runs, as the liver's glycogen stores are fast being used up, the body takes longer to break down glycogen into glucose for energy, so the body is forced to rely far more on the breakdown of fats for its fuel.

Sources of protein

ANIMAL	VEGETABLE
Meat/poultry	*Protein powder
Fish	Pulses/legumes
Eggs	Soya products, tofu
Milk/milk products	Nuts, seeds

*Note: Protein powders are used by runners who undergo dramatic weight loss; generally, this is reduced muscle mass rather than body fat so the protein powders — of which the main ingredients are usually whey protein and soy protein — are ingested to build up the muscle.

THE VEGETARIAN DIET

Because runners are generally health-conscious, many runners become vegetarians. While such a health-aware lifestyle certainly helps longevity it may not be beneficial to distance runners unless they are very careful and disciplined about their food intake — there is no doubt that distance runners need a good intake of protein (which can be lacking in a vegetarian diet). Without this it takes longer for any muscle damage to be healed and for proper post-training and racing recovery to take place.

Archaeologists and anthropologists know that hunter-gatherers of the past as well as those of our modern times were and are carnivorous. The bulk of their diet consisted of gathered foods with nearly 80 per cent being carbohydrate-laden vegetable foods. However, these hand-collected foods also included sources of protein and fat such as tortoises, lizards, the contents of birds' nests and many edible insects. Occasionally in the past they would hunt, but more often they chased off large predators from their kills by hurling sticks and rocks at them. Of significance, then, is that meat, fowl and fish were a small but important part of their diets — and evidence shows that hunter-gatherers were (and are) generally slim with very little body fat. In addition, their coronary arteries are clear and unclogged.

Many Western countries, on the other hand, are producing populations of obese, unfit individuals, the reason for which is partly the rich, fat-laden, fast-food diets they are consuming. Today's meat products are often overprocessed, contain too many chemicals, growth hormones and steroids, and also have a high fat content compared with the lean venison that hunter-gatherers eat. Therefore the vegetarian diet may be the best way for the sedentary modern individual to stay healthy. For distance runners however, with their specialized nutritional requirements, the vegetarian way of life, if too strict, may deprive them of proteins, minerals, fats and amino acids. A sensible diet free of excess fat but with a small percentage of protein appears to be the answer.

The biggest concern for vegetarians is to find suitable substitutes for meat to ensure a sufficient supply of protein and to guard against any vitamin deficiencies.

Vegans   Of the different types of vegetarian, the term vegan applies to those who eat no animal products at all. This can lead to a deficiency in calcium, vitamin B_2 (or riboflavin, which is present in organ meats, milk and eggs) and vitamin B_{12}. Vitamin B_{12} is a problem for all vegetarians as it occurs only in animal products (liver, kidneys, milk, eggs, fish).

Lacto-vegetarians   As they include dairy products in their diet, these vegetarians can obtain protein, calcium, and vitamins B_2 and B_{12} from milk-related products.

HOW TO EAT BEFORE A RACE

At least 24 hours before a race, eat foods that are a normal part of your diet and with which you are thoroughly familiar. Stay away from any foods you know could upset your digestive system. If you suffer from bowel problems, avoid high-fibre foods that contain a lot of roughage such as bran cereals, beans, and so on. Note that broccoli creates gas in the stomach.

Carbohydrate-rich foods that are good to ingest the morning of the race are raisins, bananas, bagels (which contain highly refined flour), and carbo-loaded sports drinks.

ABOVE *The nuts, oats and rice normally contained in energy bars constitute complex carbohydrates and provide a more sustained energy source than that supplied by simple sugars such as glucose.*

Energy boosts for racing

Corn syrups Specially designed for runners to easily carry during a race, corn syrups — which have the consistency of a thick, gooey gel — are packaged in small transparent or foil sachets. Extremely sweet, they provide the runner with a very high concentration of carbohydrates to give an instant energy boost. It is important, though, for runners to swallow them with water as the body will otherwise struggle to dilute the highly concentrated sugars.

The most important components of the corn syrup are maltose, maltotriose and dextrose, and maltodextrin, which is a glucose polymer (starch metabolized into glucose chains of five to 10 units). The latter are more slowly absorbed and therefore the energy they provide is more sustaining.

Simple carbohydrates such as glucose or sucrose (both of which are short-chain, quick-release carbohydrates) provide fast-releasing energy but this is not as enduring. Fructose (or fruit sugar), on the other hand, is a short-chain, slow-release carbohydrate, which provides a slower source of energy for athletes since the liver first has to convert it to glucose, which then needs to be transported to the muscles.

The foil packaging of some gels protects the syrup contents from external influences and keeps the sugars stable, while the syrups packed in plastic, if exposed to the sun, may become oxidized. If this happens, they behave more like glucose than glucose polymers.

Energy bars As an alternative in races lasting several hours, energy bars can provide a more complex, slower-release source of carbohydrates. Also very portable for runners, they are easily digestible and their carbohydrates are generally supplied in the form of oats, rice, nuts, bananas, honey, and dried fruit (raisins, sultanas). Be wary of energy bars that have a high fat content: fats are digested and absorbed slowly. Look for bars that contain, at most, 5g fat per 100g.

Lacto-ovo-vegetarians This type of vegetarian will eat eggs in addition to dairy foods, so has a similar vitamin intake to the lacto-vegetarian. Eggs are a good source of protein and vitamin B_{12}.

For vegetarians generally, sources of protein, besides dairy foods, are seeds (sunflower, sesame, poppy, linseed), nuts and soya products. Vegetarians are also prone to iron deficiency since its major sources are red meat, liver and egg yolks. It exists too in dark-green, leafy vegetables such as spinach and broccoli, nutty breads and wholegrains such as oats, wheat and rye, and raisins, but an added problem is that a high-fibre diet slows up the absorption of iron.

To ensure a well-balanced diet, true vegetarians need to combine pulses with cereal grains (wheat, maize, oats, rice). Cereals are a good source for the B-vitamin group while pulses, which derive from leguminous, or nitrogen-rich, crops, are rich in calcium and dietary fibre. Pulses include peas, lentils and dried beans — kidney, lima, haricot, black-eyed and chickpeas.

RIGHT *Raisins are an excellent source of magnesium and iron, and are high in carbohydrates (in the form of fructose sugars).*

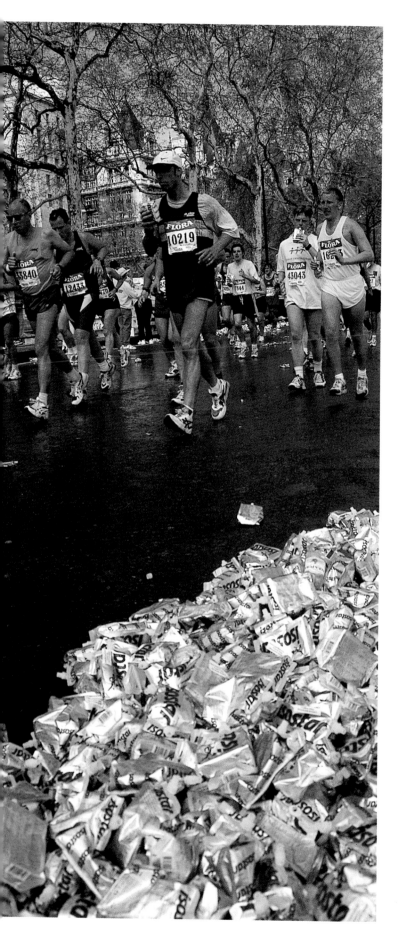

THE ROLE OF SUPPLEMENTATION

Not too long ago it was felt that athletes supplementing their diets with vitamins and minerals were wasting their money and were simply producing 'expensive urine'. Recently there has been a complete swing away from this thinking; it appears there is a major case for supplementation. There are three areas in which supplementation can aid the runner.

In Training

Training forms 80–90 per cent of a runner's programme. It is important when training for a specific event that you boost energy levels and replenish depleted nutrients to keep illness at bay and stave off bone and muscular injuries. This is particularly important during any hard training phase when many runners complain that they often wake up in the morning feeling more tired than when they went to bed the night before.

Competition

Some supplementation can actually help boost the runner while he or she is competing. Caution has to be exercised, though, because the stress of the competition coupled with the addition of supplements to the diet can result in an upset stomach.

Recovery

Supplementation plays a vital role in training- and post-race recovery. Hard running breaks the body down and sensible supplement helps it to recover. For professional runners this is very important but even those of us who run for fun want to avoid missing that very important part of our week because of injury or sickness.

Very important for post-effort recovery is omega-3, the vital oil extracted from fish like salmon and mackerel. It helps to ease tired bruised muscles, lubricates the joints and fights cholesterol, keeping the coronary arteries clear. Competing runners have found that taking omega-3 before an event can reduce muscle damage and soreness, and combats the onset of pain and stiffness.

Flavonoids are extracts of dark red, purple and blue vegetables (red cabbage, beetroot, blueberries) and fruit, and these also control the effects of muscle damage and bruising. They form part of a group of powerful antioxidants which control free radicals and prevent respiratory tract infections, to which runners are extremely susceptible after hard fast runs where heavy breathing has prevailed over a prolonged period.

LEFT *Some of the races staged in European destinations provide sachets of the sports drink Isostar, which contains sucrose and glucose polymers for energy, as well as the minerals sodium and potassium.*

ANTIOXIDANTS

Free radicals are oxygen molecules that have unpaired electrons — thus making them unstable — which circulate through the body. Because of their instability, they react swiftly with single electrons belonging to proteins, fats and DNA, but in so doing, damage the molecules and the body's cell membranes. The newly formed free radicals then set out to repeat the process, causing a chain reaction. The damage they cause renders the cells vulnerable to inflammation and infection, and also speeds up ageing and degeneration of the body. Although the body's enzymes fight the radicals, there need to be sufficient minerals present, such as zinc, copper and selenium, to do this.

Exercise, in increasing heart rate and oxygen consumption and therefore the rate at which kilojoules are burnt, also forces the body to produce more free radicals. As a result, the body suffers increased cellular damage. However, the supplementation of antioxidants can counteract the potentially harmful effects of 'oxidizing' agents. These enzymes and nutrients, particularly vitamins C and E, fight the free radicals by binding with the oxidized molecules, so stabilizing them and keeping them away from the cell walls. A good example of the effect antioxidants can have is when one cuts an avocado in half and leaves it out for a few hours. Reacting with oxygen in the atmosphere, it becomes brown; but if one sprinkles lemon juice over it, the browning is greatly reduced.

Supplementation of increased and more diverse nutrients to the various systems of the body (skeletal, muscular, circulatory, cardiovascular) allows athletes to train harder, recover faster and achieve higher levels of athletic performance. More importantly, however, they can do so with a greatly reduced risk of creating accumulated stress on the body's metabolic processes because of a badly focused diet (where the emphasis is on high-fat fried junk food or non-nutritional fast-food meals). Runners who are constantly raising their heart rate and thus consuming a continually increasing number of litres of oxygen need to be aware of combating the potential danger of oxidation.

Well-known antioxidants are the carotenoids, like the flavonoids important for combating oxidation. These are the fat-soluble pigments of dark green vegetables, such as broccoli and spinach, and all yellow, orange and red fruits and vegetables (carrots, pumpkin, tomatoes, bell peppers). They serve to lessen the incidence of cardiovascular disease, the development of cataracts, and they reduce the risk of cancer.

RIGHT *When runners undergo hard endurance exercise without the compensation of a suitable exercise-related diet, controlled supplementation of essential vitamins and minerals will help prevent illness and injury.*

VITAMINS

The body cannot function properly without vitamins, which are essential for metabolism, the working of the muscles and aiding the process that breaks down fuel for energy. They also contribute to the formation of bone and tissue. Vitamins are fat-soluble (they are absorbed and stored in the body) or water-soluble (they leave the body quickly via urine and need to be ingested more often).

Vitamin C

This is a powerful antioxidant and has been proved to prevent respiratory tract infections, particularly if an increased dose (two to three 600–1000mg tablets daily) is taken before and after a long-distance race. Large doses of this vitamin appear to help to stave off a number of different infections.

Vitamin C often occurs in combination with minerals such as iron since it aids their absorption.

Vitamin E

This is similar to vitamin C in its importance and the role that it plays in the working body. Vitamin E appears to have cell restoration qualities and is often recommended for application on skin lesions, burns and scars.

Vitamins required by the body

VITAMIN	FAT-SOLUBLE VITAMINS				
	A	D	E	K	B_1 (thiamine)
SOURCE	Dairy fats egg yolk liver fish oil dark-green and yellow vegetables	Fish–liver oils margarine fortified milk	Vegetable oils dark-green leafy vegetables wheatgerm pulses nuts	Dark–green leafy vegetables	Organ meats milk peas green beans wholegrains nuts
FUNCTION	Integrates glycogen, muscle protein	Aids metabolism of calcium and phosphate for correct levels of bone calcification	Antioxidant for polyunsaturates (fish oils), aids cell respiration	Essential for blood clotting	Major role in metabolism of carbohydrates, formation of haemoglobin

Vitamin B-complex

The B-group vitamins are good for boosting energy, especially in tired, overstrained runners. In the past many runners gave themselves B_{12} injections (this is successful in terms of giving an instant 'fix') but modern supplements are now better absorbed than in the past and more easily taken.

Vitamins B_6, B_{12} and folate are all very important to the body; B_6, particularly, is involved in the formation of the brain chemicals that boost mood and memory. B_{12} exists only in animal foods — meats, fish, eggs — which is bad news for vegetarians, while B_6 exists in liver, bananas and green leafy vegetables.

Where organ meats are mentioned, these refer to the liver, kidneys, brains, and giblets.

Cereals and wholegrains: the structure of most grain cereals consists of the hull, or outer layer, which is not eaten; bran, which is indigestible but an excellent source of vitamins and fibre; endosperm, the starch component of the grain; and the germ, which contains a high amount of fat and protein. Wholegrains and wholegrain cereals consist of all these parts with the exception of the outer hull and include corn, wheat, oats, rye, barley, and bran. Wholemeal pasta and breads, and brown rice are also wholegrains.

WATER-SOLUBLE VITAMINS

B_2 (riboflavin)	B_6	B_{12}	Folic Acid	Niacin	C (ascorbic acid)
Organ meats milk eggs dark-green leafy vegetables wholegrain cereals	Liver wholegrain cereals bananas peanuts green leafy vegetables	Organ meats poultry fish eggs milk	Organ meats eggs dark-green leafy vegetables wholegrain cereals	Meat poultry fish wholegrain cereals pulses/legumes nuts green vegetables	Citrus fruits strawberries guavas tomatoes broccoli potatoes
Essential to cell development and growth	Formation of haemoglobin, synthesizes glycogen and protein, breaks down glycogen	Development of red blood cells, metabolism of carbohydrates and fats	Important in formation of red blood cells	Plays role in production of energy (glycolysis), synthesizes fats	Stimulates production of cell collagen, antioxidant, combats infection, aids iron absorption

Major minerals required by the body

MINERAL	Sodium 500mg	Potassium 2-4g	Magnesium 300-350mg	Calcium 800-1200mg	Sulphur	Phosphorus (800mg)
SOURCE 100mg or more essential to the body daily	Salt milk meat poultry fish	Cereals fruit vegetables	Cereals nuts raisins pulses/legumes meat milk	Cheese nuts/seeds milk products oysters broccoli leafy vegetables	Meat milk cheese eggs pulses/legumes nuts	Milk eggs pulses/legumes nuts wholegrain cereals

MINERALS

Most minerals are lost through sweat, so many distance runners will take a multimineral to cover any potential losses; this will generally include potassium, zinc, copper, selenium (a by-product of copper), and even gold and nickel.

Magnesium

Correct and successful muscle contraction appears to be related to both magnesium and calcium levels within the body, so these two minerals could be involved in the prevention of cramps. Magnesium plays a role, too, in the formation of glycogen. It can be obtained from green and dried beans, the skin of potatoes, nuts and raisins. Because it exists in many foods and loss through sweat is minimal, runners shouldn't experience a deficiency in this mineral.

Calcium

The skeleton contains 99 per cent of the body's calcium, which we get from all dairy produce. Many distance runners have dangerously low bone-density, which can lead to health problems, in particular, stress fractures. It is a well-known fact in distance running that the onset of fractures can be the beginning of the end of a person's running lifestyle, particularly among female runners. Runners who don't eat enough dairy foods can build up a calcium deficiency, leading to insufficent calcification of the bones. Adding calcium to one's diet helps to build up the correct bone density.

It is not unusual for the stress of high-intensity training and a lack of calcium intake to interfere with women runners' hormonal balance, putting a stop to their menstruation cycle — a condition known as amenorrhoea. It is recommended that they include dairy products in their diet and see a gynaecologist for hormonal supplements. Vegans should ensure they take calcium supplementation.

Potassium

This mineral (together with sodium, often referred to as an electrolyte) is important for maintaining a balance in the body's fluids. It is stored in the body together with glycogen and is released into the bloodstream when the body uses its glycogen reserves for energy. The body rids itself of excess potassium through sweat and urine

MINERAL	Iron (10–18mg)	Zinc (15mg)	Copper (2mg)	Fluorine	Iodine (100–130µ)	Chromium Cobalt
SOURCE No more than a few mg per day required	Organ meats egg yolk pulses/legumes leafy vegetables prunes apricots	Meat oysters pulses/legumes wholegrains	Meat (incl. liver) shellfish pulses/legumes nuts wholegrain cereals	Drinking water	Seafood	No food source

before it does sodium chloride, and in this way guards its salt reserves. Potassium occurs in cereals, tomatoes, citrus and bananas.

Iron

Although most sedentary people do not need iron supplementation as there is generally sufficient in our diet, women are at risk because of menstruation and vegetarians, particularly, can suffer from a lack of iron because its main source is organ meats and egg yolks. Distance runners, too, may need iron at times, particularly when training exceptionally hard. Iron helps to raise the haemoglobin content (red oxygen-carrying pigment containing iron in the red blood-cells) of the blood and assists with the transport of oxygen around the body and to the working muscles. Athletes lose iron through sweat and through foot strike anaemia, a condition peculiar to runners in which they lose red blood cells through burst capillaries on the soles of their feet.

Iron is a poorly absorbed mineral and is best taken with fruit juice or vitamin C to aid absorption; many off-the-shelf products come in this combined form. Coffee and tea also hamper iron absorption. Runners who are low in iron will notice the effects of supplementation through an awareness of having more 'spring in their stride' and a greater boost of energy. The British long-distance star of the 1970s, Brendan Foster, attributed his performance improvement to iron supplementation.

Salt/Sodium

Salt (sodium chloride) is an important mineral in the body, but over the years too much emphasis has been placed on the importance of its role. Two myths associated with salt are that it can prevent cramps and that a working body requires more salt than a sedentary one. Most people consume 10 times more than their daily requirement of sodium per day, failing to realize that it is present in many of the foods we eat, especially processed foods. In actual fact, the body needs only 3g of salt per day.

Salt is important for maintaining the body's water and fluid content (the body is comprised of 60 per cent water), keeping the osmotic process in balance and setting blood pressure levels. A major drop in this percentage results in dehydration.

ALCOHOL

Many runners consume alcoholic drinks after hard running. While this may supply a quick boost of simple carbohydrates, it does little for the runner's health or recovery process since alcohol is a diuretic and dehydrates the body. Alcohol also negatively affects physical performance; it hinders the metabolism of carbohydrates and glycogen in the liver. Additionally it inhibits the absorption of vitamins, particularly B6 and thiamin, and because of its diuretic properties leaches them from the body.

On the other hand, distance runners are human, not robots, so the rewards of a rousing after-race party make the hard training and sacrifice worth the effort.

RIGHT *Contrary to the belief that taking additional salt combats cramps, as the body is exercised it loses fluid and becomes dehydrated, so the concentration of salt in fact rises in the cells.*

BELOW *The consumption of alcohol should be restricted to after – rather than before – a race!*

INJURIES

ALL INJURIES OCCUR FOR ONE OF TWO REASONS: THE RUNNER IS OVERDOING TRAINING OR THERE IS A BIOMECHANICAL-RELATED PROBLEM WITH HIS OR HER SHOES.

HOW TO AVOID INJURY

It cannot be denied that there are dangers inherent in running; certainly, with all hard physical pursuits there is always the risk of injury — and every runner will soon find out that running-related injuries are common. Most are simply caused by the overzealous (yet understandable) drive of runners who push themselves too hard, too early on in the sport. This, combined with — in some runners — poor biomechanics and an incorrect choice of footwear that offers bad cushioning and support can lead to many problems.

Learn to Run Defensively

Common to all sports is the danger of accidental injury through falling, tripping and so on. Running is a fairly controlled, fairly safe sport, but in the dark or twilight, runners nevertheless need to be constantly aware of the dangers of potholes, kerbstones and slippery surfaces (as a result of loose gravel, oil residues or ice). Happily, though, most running accidents and falls are more embarrassing than damaging. See the panel for safety tips.

Learn to Listen to your Body

The physical process of running, although ultimately health-inducing, does place stresses on your muscles and bone structure, so the combined load of a training programme together with the stress of your normal day has to be calculated. You can monitor the effect of this stress by listening to your body and noting any elevated heart rate accompanied by a shortness of breath, feelings of low energy or listlessness, a minor cough, or a sore throat. These are all minor warning signs of a potential fever or of overtraining that, if ignored, can lead to more serious problems.

Sports doctors generally take the viewpoint that if a cold is confined to the head or the sinuses, it is okay to run, but once it reaches the chest (with accompanying tightness, wheezing, and

RIGHT *Understanding and being fully in tune with your body will allow you to recognize the signs of potential injury or exhaustion early on in a race, enabling you to take measures that can alleviate your condition.*

Running safely

▸ Since most runners will run on the roads, often in high-density urbanized areas, it is essential that they learn to run defensively. They should always run on the side that faces oncoming traffic, and should look out for vehicles, both ahead and from behind, NEVER assuming that they will look out for you. Drivers can become quite aggressive and many will not give runners a wide berth.

▸ When running in a group, try not to encroach too much into the road; there is nothing more irritating to a motorist who is thus prevented from passing.

▸ Try to avoid routes that have narrow — or no — shoulders. This is particularly dangerous when cars are constantly passing each other in both directions.

▸ If running in a foreign country, be acutely aware that laws determining which side of the road to drive on may differ from those of your country. Always look in both directions before crossing a road.

▸ It often helps to wear light-coloured clothing, or an item of clothing that has reflective tape attached to it (this is a feature on many running shoes; one can also buy a reflective belt to wear around the waist).

▸ When participating in a race, be aware that danger lurks at the start when hundreds of runners can shove you out of the way (particularly when you are at the front of the starting pack). Also look out for discarded plastic bin liners (used by runners to cut out the early morning chill), crumpled T-shirts and so on at the starting area. This is also relevant during the race, particularly around the refreshment stations, where runners are constantly dropping their empty water sachets while on the run.

coughing) running should not be undertaken as this could put a strain on the heart. This is also the case with a mild temperature or any niggling aches and pains in the muscles.

The Importance of Rehydration

Anyone who has ever passed a kidney stone can attest to it being an excruciating experience. A hard mass formed in the kidney from acid salt crystals composed of calcium or uric acid in the urine, this condition has been proved to be exacerbated by dehydration — making long distance runners particularly susceptible to kidney stones. The larger stones may become lodged in the tube leading from the kidneys to the bladder. These can often be cleared by drinking a lot of water but may need to be dissolved by a prescribed medicine.

BELOW *One of the ways the body combats heat build-up during running is by increasing the circulation of blood to the skin's surface from where the heat is released by sweating. The body therefore also loses water, which needs to be replaced. In the early stages, dehydration causes a loss in concentration with a subsequent drop in the runner's performance.*

Runners should be aware of the dehydration that can result from progressive depletion of the body's reserves over weeks and months of training in hot weather, and they need to take precautions to properly rehydrate after each long training session. Most runners quickly become aware of the dangers of a hard race in hot weather, but few are aware of the problem of accumulated and progressive dehydration. Tests show that a runner can easily sweat between 1 and 2 litres (1.5 and 3.5pt) in an hour; the suggested replacement of liquids is to drink half a litre (1pt) of water for every .5kg (1lb) of moisture lost (you would need to weigh yourself before and after a run to ascertain the rate at which you sweat). Generally, the wisest practice is to put aside a suitable bottle or jug of between 500ml–1 litre (1–1½pt) of water, to be drunk at the end of every run.

RUNNING-RELATED CONDITIONS TO WATCH OUT FOR

Runners need never experience the following conditions but it is always wise to be aware of the potential for illness since recognizing early warning signs can lead to preventive measures early on rather than too late.

Blood in the Urine (Haematuria)

This is a frightening experience and if it occurs, needs to be looked into by a medical expert. However, in many runners, blood in the urine need not indicate a serious ailment; it is caused by a problem called 'bladder slap'. This occurs when the walls of the empty bladder hit each other repeatedly during running; the bruising of the bladder membrane results in the passing of red blood cells in the urine. It is important therefore that runners tell their urologist or doctor of their running activity. A solution to the problem is to consume fluids half an hour or so before a run to ensure that the bladder is half-full when starting the run, since it has been proven that the condition does not occur when the bladder is holding fluid.

Heart Attack

All intensive sport has the potential for sudden death through coronary arrest. Every runner, therefore, should have a regular, full medical check-up, and should be aware of the warning signs (a tight chest, pain on the left side, shortness of breath). A few years ago, those people opposed to running as a 'healthy' sport crowed when American Jim (James) Fixx collapsed and died at the age of 54 while out running. In the USA, Fixx was considered the guru of running, his book *The Complete Book of Running* proving to be a huge bestseller — and the dissidents of running were smug about the death of one of the disciples of modern running. What they did not consider was that Fixx had a genetic problem (his father died of a heart attack at the age of 45); he was a heavy smoker too. Running did not directly kill Jim Fixx, although while undergoing strenuous exercise his body was trying its best to warn him of an imminent problem, which he ignored. He had at some stage acknowledged a tight chest while running, and some time before his death had refused to have his heart checked. The reality is that running — and the attendant state of fitness it brought with it — probably gave him a decade longer of healthy life than his father.

Anorexia

Running often attracts the type of person who is driven and motivated, and the danger is that it can be a magnet for the anorexic personality, which manifests similar traits. Because of the modern emphasis on slimness and athletic bodies, the compulsive person — who is zealous about achieving, is highly determined and tends towards perfectionism — will be drawn to excessive exercise. Those

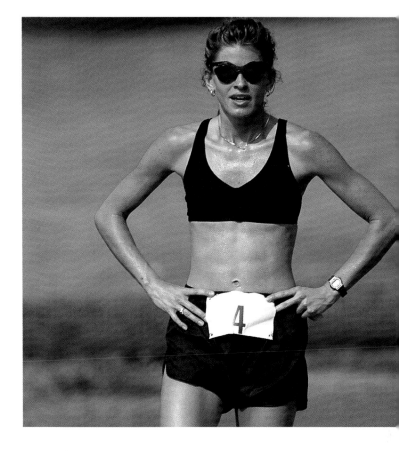

ABOVE *It is particularly important for thin runners, who have minimum fat reserves from which to draw additional energy, to ensure that they take in adequate, balanced nutrition to fuel their energy needs during training.*

who suffer from the eating disorder anorexia nervosa have a deep need to be in control; running makes them feel better about themselves and their appearance, boosting their self-confidence — and it is an activity they can regulate. However, in an added effort to prove their control they will often deny themselves small pleasures and this can lead to a fanaticism in which running on a regular basis adds to the ritualistic nature of their rigidly managed lives. The great danger, though, is that anorexic athletes eat like birds while continuing to train hard, thus severely endangering their health, and such runners need to be aware of the threat of not hitting the right balance between being high achievers and damaging their physical wellbeing. Certainly, anorexia nervosa can be treated and behavioural psychotherapy has proven effective in this regard.

TO DENY THE PRESENCE OF PAIN IS TO DENY OURSELVES THE FUN OF PAIN-FREE RUNNING.

ADVICE FOR PREVENTION OF INJURY

In most cases running injuries result from one of two causes: poor biomechanics and incorrect training during which runners tear muscles by doing speedwork or by racing without an adequate warm-up. The injuries themselves are of two types, that is, the result of extrinsic or intrinsic causes. The condition or state of your body is the influencing factor for intrinsic injuries — pronation tendencies, tight unstretched muscles, inequal length of your legs. External conditions imposed on your body result in extrinsic injuries — the way you go about your training, your choice of shoes, hard road surfaces and their camber, and so on.

In the case of biomechanics, the key is to invest in footwear that solves the problem i.e. a heavy pronator must wear a shoe that offers lots of support and cushioning to combat the pronation.

In the second instance, it is important to increase training gradually and in plateaus (see diagram below) so that the body can adapt to the ever increasing work load.

We never properly acknowledge that while the heart and cardiovascular system are able to adapt quickly and efficiently to increased training, the body's support systems do not: muscles, tendons, ligaments and bones adapt more slowly to the stress of increased training and need time to do so properly. The process cannot be hurried and often has to be almost retraced after every hard long-distance race or when we injure ourselves.

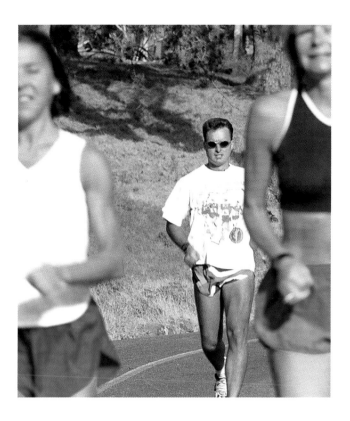

ABOVE *The key to avoiding injuries when starting out as a runner is not to push your body too hard and to pace yourself properly to allow the legs sufficient time to adjust to the sudden increase in weight-bearing exercise.*

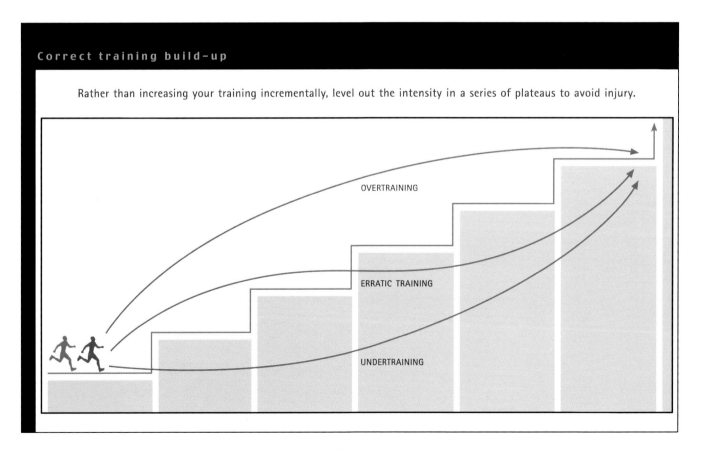

Correct training build-up

Rather than increasing your training incrementally, level out the intensity in a series of plateaus to avoid injury.

OVERTRAINING

ERRATIC TRAINING

UNDERTRAINING

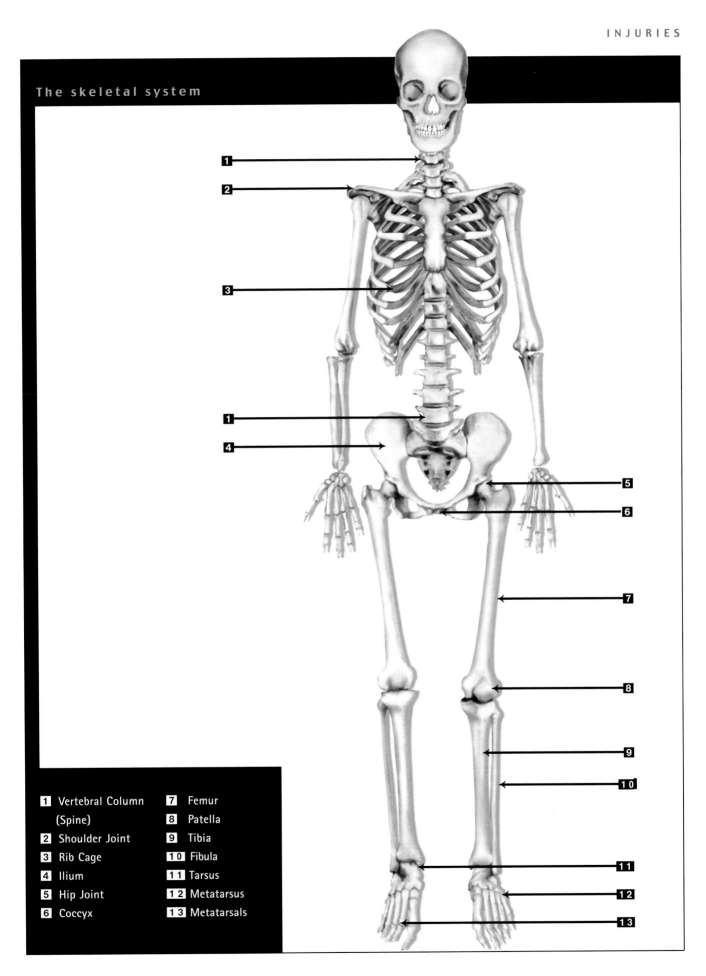

The skeletal system

1 Vertebral Column (Spine)
2 Shoulder Joint
3 Rib Cage
4 Ilium
5 Hip Joint
6 Coccyx
7 Femur
8 Patella
9 Tibia
10 Fibula
11 Tarsus
12 Metatarsus
13 Metatarsals

1 Deltoid
2 Triceps Brachii
3 Vastus Lateralis*
4 Tensor Fascia Lata
5 Adductor Longus
6 Iliotibial Band
7 Rectus Femoris*
8 Patella (kneecap)
9 Tibialis Anterior
10 Biceps Brachii

11 Gluteus Maximus
12 Semitendinosus•
13 Biceps Femoris•
14 Sartorius
15 Semimembranosus•
16 Vastus Medialis*
17 Gracilis*
18 Gastrocnemius
19 Soleus
20 Achilles Tendon

* Quadriceps   • Hamstrings

Some vital tactics for handling injury are: first, to avoid them! This is easier said than done, but if you apply the following criteria, you've got a much better chance:

Choose Footwear Carefully

Even a slightly worn heel counter which has collapsed only a millimetre or two can result in a strained Achilles tendon. Rotate shoes often, using different pairs of the same shoe model. Never hesitate to discard a pair that have reached their 'dump-by' date.

Train Sensibly

Don't rush the fitness process. Always err slightly on the side of caution when training, and force yourself to allow for rest and recovery time.

Warm up for Speed and Intensity-work Training Sessions

Don't just launch into a sprint while out on a jog. Stretch a little first; do some run-throughs, moving consistently into full speed. The same applies to hillwork. Warm up correctly beforehand.

After your speedwork and racing, jog a couple of cool-down kilometres. Never finish a run with a furious sprint as it will leave your muscles shortened and tight, although this can be alleviated to some extent by doing some long cool-down stretches after the run.

Race Sensibly

Don't over-race. Select races with care. Taper before races and allow lots of recovery time after each race. Remember that the world's leading marathon runners race two or three marathons a year and no more. We lesser runners should acknowledge that this same rule of caution applies equally to us.

If you do suffer injury, despite your best attempts to be sensible:

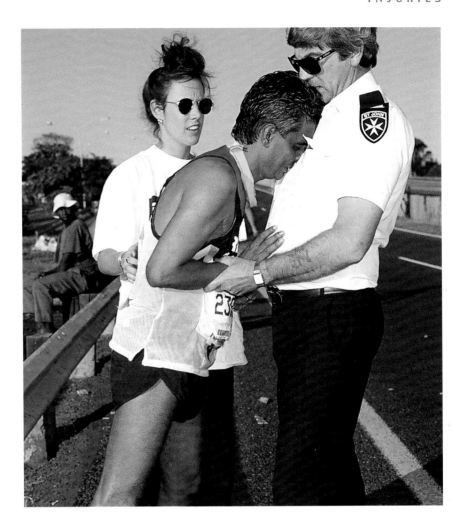

Admit that you are Injured

It may seem bizarre, but runners generally are such driven, motivated people that they tend to drive themselves on through pain, often denying that they have a problem. We all get little niggles, cramps and puzzling stabs of pain from time to time; wise runners can tell the difference between these and real injuries. Generally the serious injury is a pain that starts almost immediately after commencing running and stays with the runner throughout the training run. It may even get worse as the run progresses. It can force a runner to compensate and run with an odd gait or style. Occasionally injuries can make themselves felt but as the muscles warm up they will fade during the run; however, the fact that they are noticeable

ABOVE *Completing a marathon is the true test for the running body. When runners graduate to an ultramarathon, they push their physical abilities to their outer limits and it is inevitable that, occasionally, a point of utter exhaustion is reached – caused by factors such as dehydration, muscle glycogen-depletion, and muscle seizure.*

on every run is a warning to you. The sensible runner is mature enough to admit an injury. Immature runners deny they have a problem and believe that they can 'run through it' or that it will 'come right and eventually go away'. Ninety-nine per cent of injuries do not go away and only get worse. The mature runner gains time by not denying the injury and immediately doing something about it.

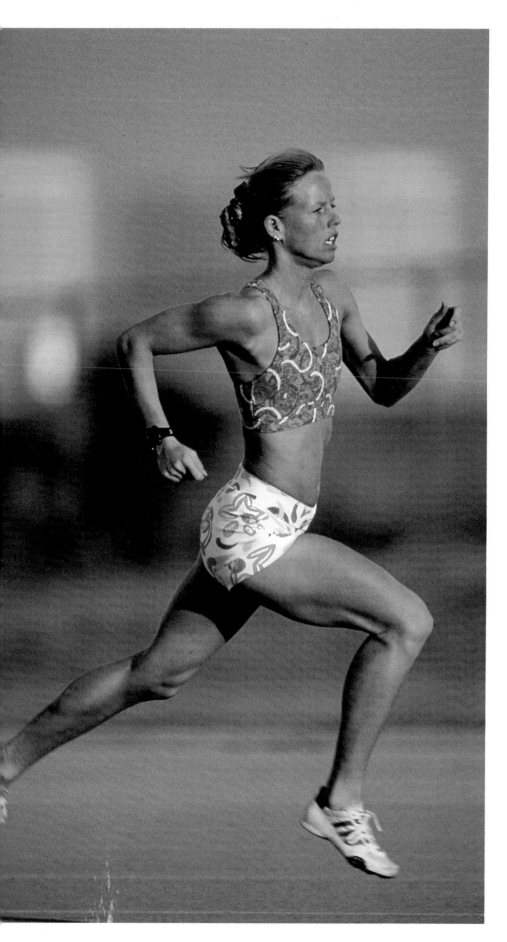

Cut Back on Training and Racing

Almost every distance runner dreads the idea of having to cut back, or worse, stop running altogether. And it is while they are forced to cut back that runners understand how important runnning is to them — take it away and they will miss it terribly. Unfortunately at times this may be necessary. A short break to aid recovery is far better than a lengthy period of enforced inactivity as a result of an injury being allowed to get worse.

In fact, in many cases, a total break from running may not be necessary. It is often sufficient to simply cut back, run slower, or stay away from steep hills. Sometimes runners may have to train on softer wood-chip trails or on grass to avoid the pounding of road-running. It is only the most serious injuries that will require total and lengthy breaks.

Seek Professional Help

Once a runner is aware of an injury, it may be necessary to seek the help of a doctor or physiotherapist. It could save time and bring about a speedier recovery to seek the help of those who specialize in sports medicine. Physiotherapists have access to a variety of techniques and machines to aid recovery. Ultrasound, massage, cross-friction (painful but effective), heat pads and many more treatments may be used in combination with rest, special exercises, new running shoes and even a changed diet to combat injuries.

Ultimately, the runner will only fool him- or herself by choosing to ignore an injury. It is better to enlist the advice of the experts.

LEFT *Whenever you incorporate a speed session into your weekly training, such as a time trial or interval training, you should turn the next run into an easy-paced session to give your muscles a rest from the increased load placed on them.*

THE MAJOR RUNNING INJURIES

Although this is not a comprehensive list of all the injuries a runner can suffer, their choice of activity does put a strain on the musculoskeletal system and there are a number of inevitable aches and pains that are common to all runners.

BONE INJURIES

The most commonly occurring bone-related conditions are shin splints and stress fractures.

SHIN SPLINTS

Shin splints (more correctly known as tibial and fibular bone strain) is a bone injury common in high-impact sports and is caused by excessive ankle pronation or the bones being subjected to excessive repeated shock. It is in fact another form of stress fracture (see p110). Occasionally the bone is not damaged but the muscles around the tibia and fibula are subjected to repeated stress from overpronation and as a result, tear and become inflamed. The pain is generally felt in one of three areas:

- ▸ to the back and inside of the lower third of the large shinbone (tibia)
- ▸ to the front of the tibia (i.e. more centralized)
- ▸ along the outside edge of the smaller shinbone (fibula)

Pain is experienced while running, but may disappear once the muscles are warmed up. If the runner perseveres, it does worsen and become more persistent. If ignored, this condition could progress from a muscular injury to a bone strain, and eventually to a stress fracture.

Common running injuries

Knee Injuries

Iliotibial Band Syndrome

Shin Splints

Plantar Fasciitis

Achilles Tendonitis

Tarsal Tunnel Sydrome

Causes

Where the injury is muscular, it is a tear in the tibialis anterior (front) or tibialis posterior (back) muscles from repeated contraction of the tibialis and soleus muscles; this results in the bony layer, known as the periosteum, becoming inflamed.

In the case of a bone strain, runners who suffer from overpronation or who suddenly increase their training programme will create a stress overload on their bones. This will inevitably lead to a weakness in the bone area.

Shin splints

Injury to back of tibia

Injury to front of tibia

Injury to outside edge of fibula

Treatment

Shin splints should be treated immediately with ice. Regular stretching of the calf muscles will ensure more flexibility in future. Speedwork and steep downhills should be avoided, and softer running surfaces selected. Take care to control overpronation; stable, corrective shoes that control foot movement should be worn. It may be necessary to wear a custom-built arch support. If the injury is a fracture, a gradual reintroduction to running is necessary after six to eight weeks of rest.

BONE STRESS FRACTURES

This is an injury to be avoided at all costs, the result of repeated stress over time on a bone in the lower limbs. The greatest percentage occurs in the tibia, with a reasonably large occurrence in the bones of the toes (metatarsals).

The pain of a stress fracture is intense and sudden and, unlike the pain of many other injuries, is impossible to overcome. While many runners can force themselves to continue running with runner's knee, iliotibial band friction syndrome (ITBS), or a minor muscle tear, running with a stress fracture is so intensely painful it is simply impossible. Slight pressure on the site of the injury is acutely sore; there is no mistaking this ailment. The injury does sometimes show up on an X-ray, but this is not always successful as the fracture is often so fine. The best indication of a stress fracture is that the runner is simply unable to run at all.

A stress fracture is the result of pronation that has caused a twisting action in the tibia and fibula which leads to tiny bone cracks and excessive loading. The pain is sharp and its whereabouts more easily pinpointed. The healing process could take between six and 12 weeks of rest and physiotherapy.

There are three major causes of stress fractures:
The first is an overload in training. As with almost all running injuries, the 'too much, too soon, too often' syndrome often results in added stresses causing a fracture. Second and third are the genetic factor and shoe choice. Certain runners have a genetically inherited propensity for stress fractures. Foot type, whether pronating or supinating, also influences injury. Differences in leg length will necessitate orthotics or shoe modification. Then, the running shoes themselves: shoes that are too hard and do not absorb shock sufficiently may result in a stress fracture.

Dietary factors can come into the equation when a runner's calcium intake is too low, resulting in weaknesses in the bone structure which can lead to fractures. If a person has a history of inadequate calcium intake from an early age, he or she is at even greater risk of developing bone fractures. Such runners show a tendency for repeated fracture-related injuries and can sadly see an end to their running career because of this. The onset of a stress fracture injury is serious and one that demands respect; your body's warnings that it is being over-trained should be heeded.

The only method of recovery is rest, and this process, which can range from six to 12 weeks, should not be hurried.

LIGAMENT AND TENDON INJURIES

These bands of tissue play an integral role in the workings of muscles and are there-fore very vulnerable to injury.

KNEE-RELATED INJURIES

This is the most common form of injury among runners, and three of the more fre-quently experienced types can be isolated: patellar tendonitis, or what is generally referred to as runner's knee (pain at the bottom of the kneecap); chondromalacia (a burning or aching at the top of and behind the kneecap); and ITBS (pain at the outer edge of the knee).

Knee problems, generally, are from an overstriding action in which the lower leg strikes the ground too far forward of the knee, allowing the runner's full body weight to come down on it, thus placing added stress on the tendon behind the knee. The lower leg should hit the ground directly below the runner in order to help absorb the body's weight.

Pain at the edges and centre of the kneecap is usually caused by the cap not tracking correctly, resulting in stretched tissue or friction between the kneecap and the leg's bone or cartilage.

RIGHT *It is important to admit defeat on a train-ing run if a pain makes itself felt progressively into the run instead of disappearing with the warming up of your muscles. This is a clear indication of a potential injury and if you act early enough you could prevent it from becoming more serious.*

There are several undeniable causes for knee injuries:

- long endurance runs using inadequately trained quadriceps
- overextending the knee on downhills
- overpronating feet, and
- the road camber and hard surfaces.

It is most important to correctly identify the knee injury type, and runners are strongly advised to consult a sports medical practitioner.

RUNNER'S KNEE (PATELLAR TENDONITIS)

This is the most often experienced running injury. Although it is popularly held that runner's knee is the wearing down of cartilage between the knee joint and the tibia/femur, a condition correctly known as chondromalacia, sports scientist Tim Noakes has documented that there is no such relation. The most intense site of pain is just below the kneecap — or at the outer edge — where the patella tendon and medial and lateral retinacula tendons attach to the kneecap. The site can be isolated by pushing up the bottom edge of the patella and squeezing immediately below it. The pain usually becomes more uncomfortable with time; if the knee is bent for long periods of sitting, discomfort increases. The pain is particularly bad in very long races.

Causes

The direct cause of the injury is excessive ankle pronation or running knock-kneed. This creates a twisting force to the knee and causes stress on the kneecap's anchoring ligaments.

Treatment

Firmer, more supportive shoes can help the problem by preventing overpronation of the ankle. As with so many injuries, reducing the training load also helps to control the problem. Avoid running continually on the same side of a cambered road.

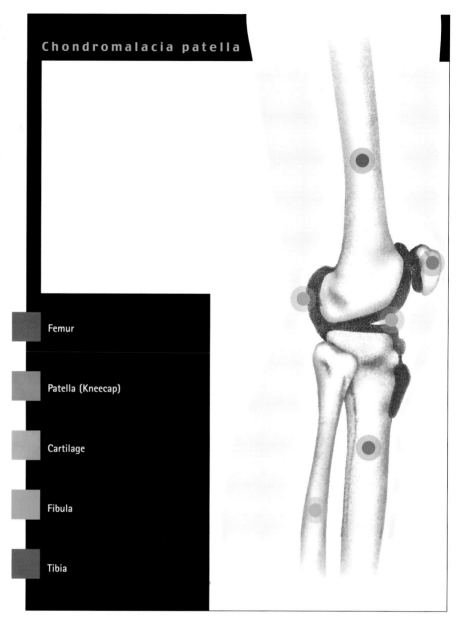

Chondromalacia patella

- Femur
- Patella (Kneecap)
- Cartilage
- Fibula
- Tibia

CHONDROMALACIA PATELLA

In this knee injury pain is felt on top of and behind the kneecap, due to the gradual wearing down of the protective cartilage which results in inflammation of the area. The runner may experience a clicking sensation or a roughness in the knee. In most cases, if left unattended this injury eventually leads to arthritis.

Causes

Again, a runner's tendency to pronate, undeveloped quadriceps — which if strong aid in the tracking of the kneecap — and training imbalances such as cambered surfaces, hills and overtraining all lead to this condition.

Treatment

The knee should be iced for around 15 minutes up to three times a day; sports stores stock flexible gel packs which are suitable for this purpose. In the worst case scenario, a surgical procedure may be necessary. This involves scraping of the patella to clear away the abrasions.

ILIOTIBIAL BAND FRICTION SYNDROME (ITBS)

This horrific-sounding injury is one encountered fairly often among runners during fairly intensive training. It is common but can be treated and is not as nightmarish an injury as its name suggests.

The iliotibial band (ITB) is a strip of tendon that extends from the hip across the outside of the knee to insert into the tibia (shin bone) immediately below the knee joint. The band can rub across the outer surface of a bony bump at the outside of the knees causing inflammation or ITB tendonitis. The injury is quite painful but very localized, just at the site of the iliotibial band's crossing of the bone. The pain only appears when the athlete is running and causes him or her to run in a stiff-legged way to avoid the pain. Downhill running is particularly painful, but the athlete can usually walk pain-free.

I am able to diagnose the injury very speedily — I simply apply pressure to the outside of the leg on the side of the knee and the injured runner will yelp in pain.

Causes

Usually the injury is a combination of too rapid an increase in training and excessive downhill running, or due to a runner's biomechanics. It exists in runners whose running shoes are too hard and therefore do not provide adequate shock absorption or in supinating runners who may also be bow-legged and have high arches to their feet. In this case, orthotic modification that serves to guide the foot inward may solve the problem.

Treatment

Immediate treatment is to ice the affected area, apply anti-inflammatory medication and rest. Runners should reduce their training, keeping away from downhills and trying out softer training surfaces. They should then try out softer, more shock-absorbing running shoes or have an expert recommend orthotics. It can help to run on the opposite side of the road to that most used in training and racing, as there seems to be a correlation between the camber of the road and the leg displaying iliotibial band friction syndrome.

Lateral stretching of the knee may also help and for healthy runners is certainly a good exercise to perform regularly to keep the iliotibial band elastic and supple. To stretch an injured IT band on

BELOW *During a race, many muscular pains can be alleviated by vigorous massage which serves to relax the contracted muscle out of its spasm. Trained staff are in many cases on hand to help.*

the left-hand side, cross your left leg behind your right one, placing your full weight on the left leg. Push your hips to the left, then clasp your hands and raise your arms, stretching them with your upper torso to the right. This creates a good stretch along your left side. Reverse the process for an injured right IT band.

ITB syndrome is a particularly difficult injury to treat, and runners should try to prevent it at all costs. While they should avoid going 'under the knife', this is one injury which, if it persists, can be helped by a simple operation. It can be done with a local anaesthetic and requires six weeks or so of rest followed by a gradual reintroduction to running.

South African marathon runner Bernard Rose struggled with iliotibial band friction syndrome. He caused a stir when in 1985 he ran two marathons back-to-back in 2:14 where one was at altitude (a 2:14 run at altitude is equal to 2:09 at sea level). Rose subsequently had both knees operated on, with excellent results.

ACHILLES TENDONITIS

The Achilles tendon attaches the calf muscles (gastrocnemius and soleus) to the heelbone (calcaneus) and acts to lift and lower the heel during walking and running. A stiffness at the back of the ankle just above the heel first thing in the morning generally brings this injury to the attention of runners.

A bruised Achilles tendon does often improve during the run once warmed up, but if ignored it can partially or fully rupture; a ruptured tendon will require surgery.

By pinching the Achilles tendon, the acuteness of the pain generally indicates the extent of the injury.

Iliotibial band friction syndrome

Biceps Femoris

Quadriceps

Iliotibial Band

Patella

Tibia

Fibula

Gastrocnemius

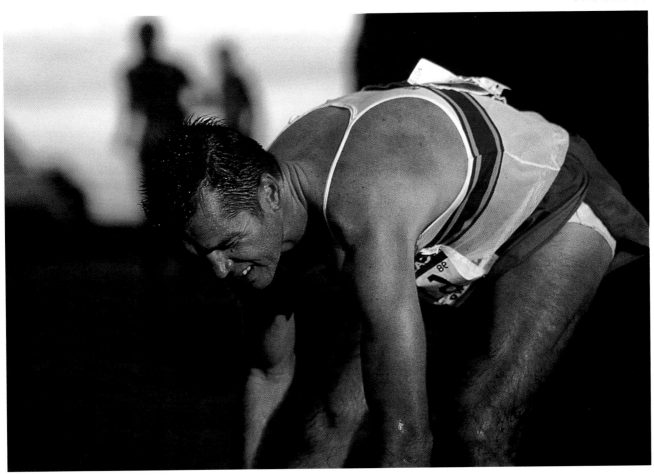

ABOVE *Injuries to the Achilles tendon are commonly experienced by a multitude of runners. In mature runners, a loss of muscle elasticity has also been known to contribute to this injury.*

Causes

Particularly after a break in training, a sudden increase in distance running or intense hill and speedwork can bring on this injury. Unfit or overtired calf muscles will pass on the load from running to the Achilles tendon. Excessive pronators who are wearing incorrect footwear or supinators with high-arched feet that are bad at shock absorption are also at risk.

Treatment

Ice the affected area immediately after a run (or daily if not running) for as much as half an hour if it's possible. Running can continue through minor pain only if it has been established that the tendon is not ruptured, but stay away from hills and reduce speed. More corrective shoes should also be looked at. Sometimes there is scarring of the tendon which can interfere with its surrounding sheath; in this case, a surgical procedure will clear the scarring.

The Chink in Achilles' Armour

In Greek mythology, Achilles, who was the son of Peleus and the sea goddess Thetis, was the greatest and fastest warrior among the Greeks at Troy. He is described as a hero in the *Iliad*, a famous work by the poet Homer. Legend relates how Achilles' mother lowered him into the Styx, the great river of the Underworld, rendering his entire body invulnerable to hurt and injury. However, in holding him by the back of his heel, this was the only area not immersed in the river's waters.

During the Battle of Troy, Achilles killed Hector, the son of Troy's king, Priam. In revenge, Hector's brother, Paris, fired an arrow which pierced Achilles' heel — the only unprotected, and most vulnerable, part of his body. This has since given rise to the much-used term 'Achilles heel' which is applied to a person's physical or psychological weak point.

PLANTAR FASCIITIS

This is a common injury which presents itself as extreme pain in the inner heel, located in the plantar fascia — a fibrous band of tissue running along the underside of the foot from the heel to the ball of the foot. It is felt during running but also first thing in the morning, when the tissue is tight. Runners tend to hobble back on their heels to find relief.

Causes

The injury appears to be prominent in chronic pronators. Because of the pronation, the plantar fascia is stretched too severely, thus becoming inflamed.

Once again, training too hard, too often, can also be a cause.

Treatment

To bring immediate relief, the plantar fascia should be iced regularly. The runner should cut back on excessive training and should avoid speedwork and hills for a while. Shoes that control excessive pronation should be worn. Stretching the calf muscles has been known to help; many runners suffering from this injury have shown a weakness in this area (too-tight calf muscles will put an added strain on the tissue of the underside of the foot).

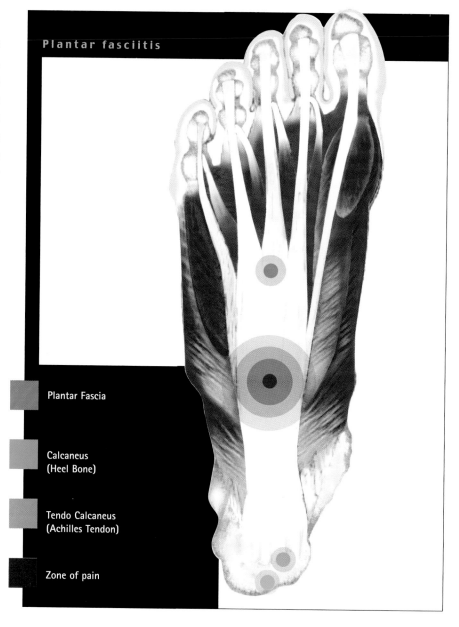

Plantar fasciitis

Plantar Fascia

Calcaneus (Heel Bone)

Tendo Calcaneus (Achilles Tendon)

Zone of pain

Tarsal tunnel syndrome

- Posterior Tibial Nerve
- Right Tarsal Tunnel
- Calcaneus (Heel Bone)
- Flexor Retinaculum

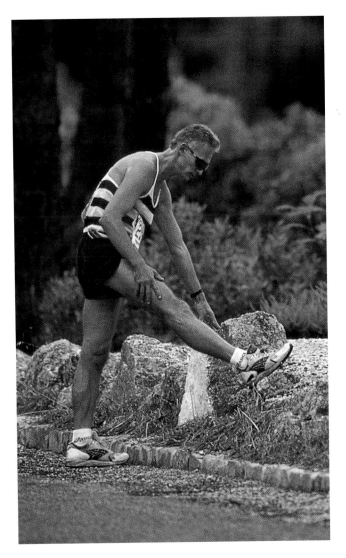

TARSAL TUNNEL SYNDROME

A relatively newly recognized condition, the importance of this injury is that it manifests itself in various other running ailments — such as shin splints, Achilles tendonitis and plantar fasciitis — because the body instinctively compensates for the discomfort it is undergoing. A pain on the inside of the ankle extending down along the arch and underside of the foot is an indication of tarsal tunnel syndrome. The injury is an irritation of the posterior tibial nerve which runs along the inside of the ankle; it is similar to the wrist pain experienced from prolonged use of a computer mouse or typing at a keyboard. As the injury worsens, the runner also experiences burning and tingling. It can be tested by pressing behind the ankle bone for any pain. A sports medicine doctor will need to carry out special nerve-conduction tests to confirm the injury.

Cause

The main cause is excessive pronation or insufficient support for the foot arch.

Treatment

Shoes may need to be adapted for pronation using arch supports or orthotics. Physiotherapy will relieve pain and irritation. In the worst case, surgery may be necessary.

LEFT *The feet — heel and arch particularly — work hard in terms of balance, carrying the body's weight, and cushioning the legs and ankles against impact.*

MUSCLE INJURIES

With the constant elongating and contracting of muscles that runners impose on their bodies, it is inevitable that overstretching and tearing occurs. Generally, muscle injuries fall into the following categories.

Strains This occurs when a muscle (or tendon) is pulled, twisted or tears and is often the result of simply not warming up the muscles through stretching for 10 or 15 minutes of slow gentle running before placing them under stress. Badly (or chronically) strained muscles can be the end result of several years of non-stretching and the mismanaged stress-loading of muscles.

Sprains When the ligament fibres of a joint are stretched beyond their limit they tear, resulting in a sprain, which is more serious than a strain. Blood permeates the tissue around the joint, creating discoloration and uncomfortable swelling. The muscle tear can be felt as a knot at the location of the pain, and will be tender when touched.

Spasms (or Cramping) This condition is caused by exercising harder than normal or running further than the runner has been used to, which creates an excessive load on the muscle. A cramp is an acute and sudden, extremely painful contraction during which the muscle bulges in a hard fibrous knot. The spasm is maintained until the fibres are forcibly relaxed through massage, stretching or they come out of the spasm naturally with the removal of the stress that initially caused it.

Cramping is the body naturally reacting to protect the joint by preventing any further motion and therefore any friction. It could also come about through a lack of glycogen in the muscle.

More specifically, muscle injuries can be divided into three types:

DELAYED MUSCLE SORENESS

A stiffness is felt in the muscles as much as 24–48 hours after a runner has done more severe exercise than normal. The affected muscles are painful when stretched, signalling that they have been stressed. The generally held belief — still being put forward in literature and running magazines — is that this is due to a build-up of lactic acid in the muscles, which is quite incorrect (see panel at right). In reality, it is a sign of damaged supporting (connective) tissue in the muscle cells.

Prevention

Runners would need to focus on additional long-distance training and work on their downhill running. The quadriceps can be strengthened through weight training.

Myths about lactate and lactic acid

Misperceptions concerning muscle stiffness after bouts of increased exercise — still being attributed to a build-up of lactic acid in the muscle cells — are still perpetuated in running books and magazines. In an effort to dispel this myth, it is necessary to go back to the early research carried out by sports scientists. At the time, lactic acid was an easily measurable chemical in the body and as it was so pervasive, it was eventually held responsible for most muscle-related injuries. Scientists put forward the theory that muscles only produced lactic acid when there was not enough oxygen for them to work aerobically, thus forcing them to function anaerobically. More recent studies have shown that lactic acid is produced even when there is a good supply of oxygen present. It exists normally in the body in the form of sodium lactate, commonly referred to as lactate.

Lactate is produced during the breakdown of carbohydrates into glycogen (glycolysis), which provides the muscles with energy; so, as carbohydrates are burned for this energy, the lactate rises in proportion to the increase in exercise. During extreme exercise, glycolysis produces acidic hydrogen ions (H-ions) as well as higher lactate concentrations; the high H-ions in the muscles prevent them from working efficiently. Lactate transports the acidic ions out of the muscle into the bloodstream.

Studies published in the *American Journal of Physiology* (E Peters-Futre et al 1987) — in which Tim Noakes was involved — and *Medicine and Science in Sports and Exercise* (J A Schwane et al 1983) proved that runners who had undergone an intense training session which would have raised their lactate levels to the maximum limits, had normal, low lactate levels an hour after the session. It is also clear that the longer races which produce the most muscle fatigue are generally run at speeds that don't actually cause a rise in lactate levels in the blood. The conclusion was reached that lactate has no relation to muscle fatigue; this increases instead when an excessive number of acidic ions is produced during the burning of carbohydrates for energy. The stiffness felt after hard exercise is the result of damaged muscle cells and connective tissue.

ACUTE MUSCLE TEAR

The runner experiences an involuntary, sharp pain during which the muscle goes into spasm and prevents the athlete from continuing any further. There will be swelling and in some cases, a bruising of the skin. This injury arises from runners neglecting to warm up sufficiently before exercising, inflexibility of the muscles, and opposing muscle groups that are not matched in strength.

Treatment

Ice the injured muscle to reduce the inflammation and try to keep the affected leg raised (alleviating the pumping action of blood to the injury and reducing pressure around it). Rest of six to eight weeks may be necessary, but treatment by a sports doctor combined with stretching and strengthening exercises has proven to speed up recovery.

INSIDIOUS MUSCLE TEAR

As its name implies, the injury begins with slight pain after a run which later makes itself felt during the run and eventually becomes so painful that training becomes difficult. The pain is acute, felt deeply within one of the major muscle groups, and usually disappears while at rest. If you feel the injury with two fingers you can usually identify a knot, formed from scar tissue and very sore to the touch. It is usually caused by intensive speedwork and particularly hard long-distance training which puts a heavy load on the muscles. I personally suffer from painful muscle tears in the soleus (calf) muscles as soon as I start intensive Comrades training, which can hamper correct training.

Treatment

Unfortunately the only successful method of treatment for this injury — cross-friction applied by a physiotherapist — is agonizingly painful. The scar tissue is rubbed vigorously over five to 10 sessions, with each one lasting up to 10 minutes.

SHOULD YOU RUN WITH AN INJURY?

Sports medicine doctors generally recommend that athletes continue with their running only if the pain is merely annoying and below your normal pain threshold. It is a fact that an injury can benefit by the increased blood supply that is generated through exercise; it also serves to carry away bruised and dead cells i.e. improved 'waste' removal.

BELOW *Any tears in the leg muscles should be taken seriously by runners and given adequate time to recover. Being negligent about this could force you out of training for up to two months if the tear is severe enough — a situation that is intensely frustrating for all runners!*

THE MARATHON AND BEYOND

IF YOU RACE A MARATHON ONCE OR TWICE A YEAR, YOU WILL RUN BRILLIANTLY
EVERY TIME. RACE MORE OFTEN, AND YOUR PERFORMANCES WILL BE MEDIOCRE.

FROM HALF TO ULTRAMARATHON

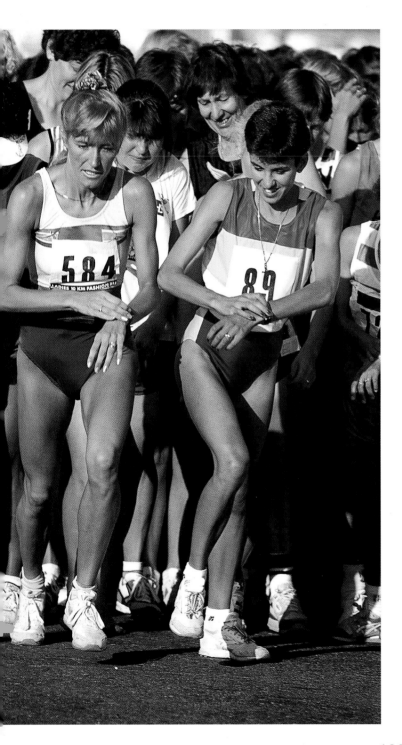

THE HALF MARATHON

Once distance runners have mastered the art of running 10km (6 miles), it is a logical step to move up to the half marathon, and later the full marathon, distance. Runners who are capable of running 10km comfortably can certainly meet the challenge of both the half and full marathon. Obviously more training is required, but the commitment is not vastly different from that of a 10K runner.

Runners should note, however, that a half marathon is not just double a 10km (6-mile) race plus 1km (half a mile). Nor is a marathon a race of four 10km segments and a bit. They are both tougher challenges. The second half of a half marathon begins at 15 or 16km (9 or 10 miles) while the second half of a full marathon begins at 30km (18½ miles). Assuming one has completed a 10km (6-mile) race fairly comfortably, the jump up to a half marathon should take about two months; a full marathon should take another two months or so.

While in training for a half marathon, always be aware of injury, and progress slowly, remembering to build up in steps and plateaus rather than in a continual upward curve (see diagram on p104).

It is important to realize that runners do not have to run 21km (13 miles) in one training session in order to race that distance. They will build up the necessary endurance in the continued and sustained training of the weeks prior to the half marathon race. At the same time, resting up before the race will also ensure that a runner has the right strength and endurance for when it matters.

A typical week of training for a half marathon should include a strength run, a semi-long run, a longer run, and a day's rest (see training table on p124).

TOP *All race entrants are required to wear an official race number, which usually displays the sponsor's name, for the duration of the event.*
LEFT *Elana Meyer (right), South Africa's most visible woman runner, is today the country's highest ranked distance runner in the international arena.*
RIGHT *In most of the large race events, every runner who finishes the half or full marathon within the official cut-off time receives a medal.*

Training schedule for a half marathon

	SIX WEEKS TO GO	FOUR WEEKS TO GO	LAST WEEK
Monday	Rest	Rest	Rest
Tuesday	8km (5 miles)	8km (5 miles)	8km (5-mile) jog
Wednesday	12km (7 miles) as a semi-long run	12km (7 miles) as a semi-long run	8km (5-mile) jog
Thursday	8km (5 miles)	8km (5 miles)	5km (3 miles) very easy
Friday	10km (6 miles) as a steady pace on a hilly course	10km (6 miles) as a steady pace on a hilly course	Rest
Saturday	5km (3 miles) as an easy run	5km (3 miles) as an easy run	Rest
Sunday	15km (9 miles) as a slow run	16–18km (10–11 miles) as a slow run	RACE DAY

The three most important factors of this training schedule are: to stick to your one day's rest per week, to slowly increase the length of your long weekend run but *not* necessarily to half marathon distance, and to completely lay off running for two days before the race so that your muscles are fresh and rested.

MARATHON

The 42.2km (26.2-mile) marathon is the 'holy grail' of every distance runner, fast or slow. To be able to say with pride, 'I am a marathoner', is one of sport's great boasts. Virtually anyone who is of reasonable health can complete a marathon, although genetic factors will determine whether it is a fast or a slow one. Training factors, on the other hand, will determine whether the marathon is going to be tough and very painful — or simply tough.

American Frank Shorter (1972 Olympic Marathon champion) has said that there is no such thing as an easy marathon; he is right. Whether run slowly or quickly, 42km (26 miles) hurts — but the hurt is nothing compared to the satisfaction of finishing the race. Most first-time marathoners experience an emotional high as they finish, with many a male hulk shedding a tear or two.

Before tackling a full marathon, some runners try a 30 or 32km (18½- or 20-mile) race, but the step up from the half marathon distance is much the same. If the half marathon effort was a hard one, it is important to recover fully before building up over about two months to the full marathon (see table on p127).

For a first marathon, it is important to choose one that offers as much support to your hard-working body as possible. In other words, stay away from obscure, hilly, hot marathon courses run at altitude. Choose a race that will be run at sea level, in cool conditions, and on as flat a course as possible. Choose one of the bigger, more famous races with lots of crowd support and a large field of runners. (You are going to need all the support and encouragement you can get!)

Do not be too concerned about your time. You will improve as you become a more experienced marathoner. Rather aim to enjoy the experience as much as possible — there simply is nothing quite like your first marathon.

There is no doubt that the marathon is a major challenge and there is much work to be done once you have completed half that distance. Those who can run a half marathon in reasonable comfort can probably get to 30km (18½ miles) without changing their training radically. However, it is the last 12km (7 miles) for which much work is required. Marathoners talk of 'hitting the dreaded wall' (see p78). There is no need for any runner to experience this, but if you are poorly trained and poorly paced, it is more than possible that you will hit that wall. (This is the point when all energy drains from the marathoner and running is like trying to swim through thick mud.)

Make sure that your body has recovered adequately from its half marathon effort before you build up to the full 42km (26-mile) distance. After that, it is consistency and regularity of training that helps to condition the body for the race. If you are carrying any additional weight, this comes off and is replaced by lean muscle.

It is very important to always be cautious. Never fight an injury (the injury will win!) and always be prepared to rest if sore legs and general lethargy prevail. If there are any doubts about how you are feeling, such as lethargy, a sore throat, heavy tired legs, immediately take a day off. Taking extra doses of vitamin C at any signs of a scratchy throat is a good precaution at this time.

It is very important to taper in the last weeks in order to arrive at the start line feeling strong and ready to race.

LEFT AND RIGHT *Running a race in a foreign land enables you to keep fatigue at bay by focusing on beautiful scenery or famous landmarks instead of on the kilometre/mile marks and on the distance; the New York Marathon crosses some famous bridges, among them the Verrazano Bridge (left).*

TAKING YOUR RUNNING FURTHER

Once you have taken the step to run a marathon, it is generally at this point that you will also want to improve on your running speed and overall performance. It has been widely proven that running at different paces in your weekly training sessions — rather than at a steady, constant speed — has the most beneficial results. At this stage it is the quality of the training, not the distance achieved, that is important.

A good way to start is to combine some interval training (see later) with an easy run before and after the intense workout. In addition, try to incorporate into each training week a mix of the following paces: easy or relaxed long runs at below 65 per cent maximum heart rate; 5–7km (3–4 miles) at your 10km (6-mile) race pace; and 8–11km (5–7 miles) at a constant half-marathon pace (tempo runs). Varying your pace from run to run trains your body to adjust to different work intensities, and conditions it to work as efficiently as possible for each.

Chapman's Peak Drive, where the road drops vertically to the Atlantic, distracts runners from the gruelling 56km (35 miles) of the Two Oceans ultramarathon.

To calculate maximum heart rate (see p60 to measure your pulse):

For women: 226 - your age = max heart rate

For men: 220 - your age = max heart rate

To calculate a percentage (e.g. 65%) of this:

max heart rate - resting heart rate x 0.65 + resting heart rate = 65% max heart rate

With your next aim fixed firmly on the marathon, a solid base needs to be developed in terms of strength and endurance. Be prepared to have some bad days, and accept that you won't always perform at your peak. Experienced runners give themselves five to 10 minutes at the beginning of a run to test the 'spring in their stride'; if their legs still feel leaden and tired, they stop running.

In order to incorporate strength-building into your weekly training, the following techniques are recommended:

▸ a 30-minute interval training session that incorporates around 10 minutes hard running, then sessions of running for five minutes at 10km (6-mile) effort with two to five minutes of recovery jogging in-between

▸ hill training

▸ for two days of the week, 25- to 40-minute runs run at a slow pace (you should feel as if you're tripping over your own feet)

Training schedule for a full marathon

	Monday	Tuesday	Wednesday	Thursday	Friday	Saturday	Sunday
Week 1	Rest	8km (5 miles)	12km (7 miles)	8km (5 miles)	10km (6 miles) hilly run	5km (3 miles)	15km (9 miles)
Week 2	Rest	8km (5 miles)	12km (7 miles)	8km (5 miles)	10km (6 miles) hilly run	5km (3 miles)	18km (11 miles)
Week 3	Rest	8km (5 miles)	12km (7 miles)	8km (5 miles)	10km (6 miles)	5km (3 miles)	20km (12 miles)
Week 4	Rest	8km (5 miles)	15km (9 miles)	8km (5 miles)	12km (7 miles) hilly run	5km (3 miles)	30 km (18½ miles)
Week 5	Rest	10km (6 miles)	15km (9 miles)	10km (6 miles)	12km (7 miles) hilly run	5km (3 miles)	20km (12 miles)
Week 6	Rest	10km (6 miles)	15km (9 miles)	10km (6 miles)	12km (7 miles) hilly run	5km (3 miles)	30km (18½ miles)
Week 7	Rest	10km (6 miles)	15km (9 miles)	10km (6 miles)	10km (6 miles) hilly run	5km (3 miles)	25km (15½ miles)
Week 8	Rest	8km (5 miles)	10km (6 miles)	8km (5 miles)	8km (5 miles) hilly run	5km (3 miles)	15km (9 miles)
Week 9	Rest	10km (6 miles) light jog	5km (3 miles) light jog	Rest	Rest plus carbo-load	Rest plus carbo-load	RACE

▶ a long endurance run, done at an easy pace, over the weekend, building up to around one and a half hours in length

▶ a day's rest: training at this constant pace greatly increases the risk of injury, so it is absolutely essential to rest your muscles

To improve on speed, try out the following tactics:

▶ Replace hill repeats with fast repetitions ranging between 200 and 1000m (220 and 1100yd). Run slightly faster than your 5km (3-mile) pace for two minutes with a minute of recovery in-between. Eventually work up to 8 to 12 repeats. At this point, you should be aiming at decreasing your recovery time

▶ The week before your first half marathon race, cut your long weekend run, interval training and hillwork by half.

PRE-RACE DAY PREPARATION

Assuming that you have already experienced your first 10K race and are familiar with the rituals of clothing, race numbers, food/snacks, and watering tables (aid stations), a few basic requirements need to be focused on for a race as long and as testing as a marathon. Every marathon runner, especially the novice, needs to be ready to race, with all equipment ready, tried and tested.

Torture-tested Equipment

It is a golden rule that on race day nothing should be new or untried. Despite the strictness of this rule, it is interesting how many runners, even experienced ones, will try something new in the hope that it will propel them to an easier, faster race. Almost always the new item conspires with the runner's foolishness to ensure that their race is not a success. Everything should be 'torture tested' prior to race day. Confidence in one's equipment is as important as training correctly. There must be no decision to make. Every item, from racing shoes to one's race watch should have been purchased way in advance. (Ensure your watch is fitted with working batteries — don't make the mistake I once did when, during the course of a crucial race, my batteries gave out!) And, needless to say, shoe choice is of paramount importance.

BELOW *The end of the race: runners will need to ensure that they replace the glycogen stores that have been depleted in the liver and muscles. Preferably eaten within the first two hours, snacks could include bananas, a peanut butter sandwich, four rice cakes with jam or honey, or muesli bars and a piece of fruit.*

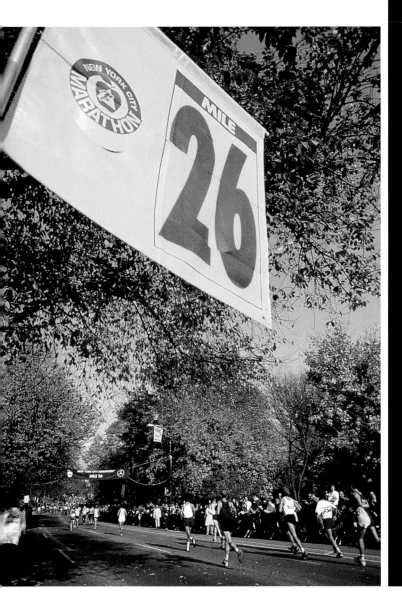

Race time comparative chart

5km (3 miles)	10km (6 miles)	15km (9 miles)	21.1km (13.1 miles)	42.2km (26.2 miles)
18:59	39:58	61:50	1:29:10	3:08:17
19:17	40:38	62:52	1:30:40	3:11:32
19:36	41:19	63:56	1:32:14	3:14:53
19:56	42:02	65:03	1:33:51	3:18:21
20:17	42:46	66:11	1:35:31	3:21:57
20:38	43:31	67:23	1:37:15	3:25:41
21:00	44:18	68:37	1:39:03	3:29:34
21:22	45:07	69:53	1:40:55	3:33:35
21:46	45:58	71:13	1:42:51	3:37:46
22:10	46:51	72:36	1:44:52	3:42:06
22:36	47:46	74:02	1:46:57	3:46:38
23:02	48:42	75:31	1:49:07	3:51:21
23:29	49:42	77:04	1:51:23	3:56:15
23:58	50:43	78:41	1:53:46	4:01:23
24:27	51:48	80:22	1:56:13	4:06:44
24:58	52:55	82:08	1:58:47	4:12:20
25:30	54:05	83:58	2:01:28	4:18:11
26:04	55:18	85:54	2:04:16	4:24:18
26:39	56:35	87:54	2:07:14	4:30:45
27:15	57:55	1:30:01	2:10:19	4:37:30
27:54	59:19	1:32:14	2:13:34	4:44:36
28:35	60:47	1:34:33	2:16:58	4:52:04
29:18	62:20	1:37:00	2:20:14	4:59:56
30:02	63:58	1:39:34	2:24:21	5:08:15
30:49	65:41	1:42:17	2:28:20	5:17:01
31:38	67:29	1:45:09	2:32:33	5:26:19

The useful table featured above can serve as a relatively accurate gauge of your projected running paces over various race distances.

If you have recorded the time that you take to complete a 10km (6-mile) course, find that pace in the relevant 10km column and read horizontally across the columns to find out how you are likely to perform in your half or full marathon. By the same token, if you improve your time over 10km, you can then see how much better you can fare over the longer distances.

By kind permission: Bobby McGee, *Runner's World*

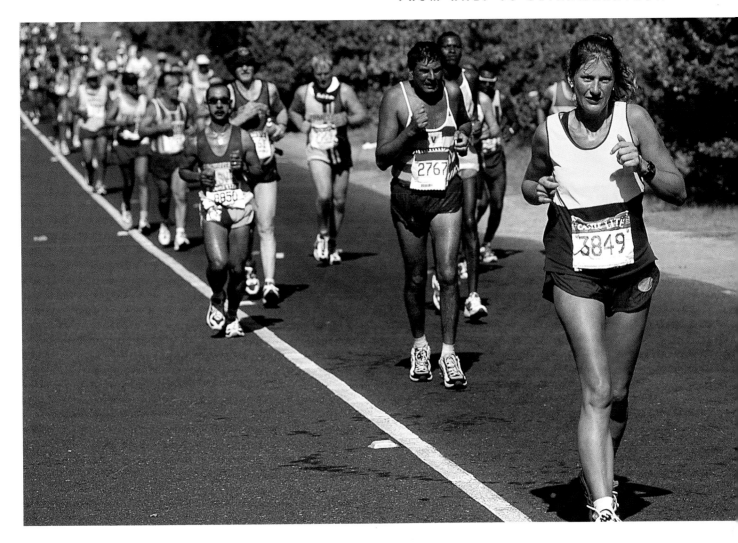

Drive the Course

If it is possible, a drive over the marathon course can be very useful. It's a sober reminder of how long the race really is and instils a sense of caution in you as a runner, so that you start slowly and build on that in the race. Knowing the course a little better can also, during the race, be encouraging to a tired runner who begins to recognize landmarks that signify the end of the race is drawing nearer. The best option of all is if you have the opportunity before race day to run along the course and so become familiar with the challenge ahead — particularly the more difficult second half.

Visualization and Motivation

As one gets fitter it becomes possible to visualize oneself on race day, especially when the race route is familiar. While training, many runners (myself included) can see themselves on specific sections of the course, running strongly. Don't visualize the impossible, seeing yourself sprinting along — rather, running strongly and confidently. It is also important to be realistic; sometimes during a training run,

ABOVE *Runners often fear that they will not be able to run beyond marathon distance. But the mind is such a powerful tool that, in a longer race, it programmes us not to view the 26-mile (42km) marker as the 'end' of the race; instead, we surprise ourselves by having the stamina for the increased distance.*

imagine the difficult mileage sections of your upcoming race i.e. 32km (20 miles) onwards in the marathon; visualize how you are handling the inevitable fatigue on that particular stretch.

To further inspire you, it can also help to study videos and film footage of the race or of other marathons. Dustin Hoffman's role in the film *Marathon Man* shows how thousands of aspiring marathoners have watched the magical film footage of Ethiopian Abebe Bikila's fine runs in the 1960 and 1964 Olympic Marathons.

Other marathoners like to listen to inspiring music and may have a theme tune that they play regularly to energize them ahead of race day, or which they can hum to themselves as they start the race. Certainly, this has worked very well for me in the past.

CARBO-LOADING AND PRE-RACE MEALS

For detailed advice on carbohydrate loading before a major race, refer to the chapter on Nutrition and Diet. But in general, while you're tapering your daily training before the Big Race, bear in mind that you should also reduce your energy intake accordingly so as not to gain weight. Try reducing your kilojoule/calorie intake by roughly 400kJ, or 100 calories, per 1.5km (1 mile) you run less. However, you still need to stock up your glycogen stores in your liver and muscles, so stick with carbohydrates such as wholegrain breads, cereals and pastas as well as fruit and vegetables. Sports nutritionists suggest that during the last three days before the race, carbohydrates should increase from 65 per cent to make up as much as 90 per cent of your diet. You may also be carbo-loading with special sports drinks during this time. Runners who need to travel long distances for the race usually have difficulty in maintaining a suitable pre-race diet. Try to get around this by taking along your own high-fibre energy bars, dried fruit, cereals and fruit/sports drinks. The day before, avoid untested foods and those with a high roughage content to prevent potential bowel problems. Drink a lot of fluids — a light-coloured urine will indicate that you are drinking sufficiently.

You should eat your pre-race meal (bananas, bagels, and even rice have all proven excellent for athletes) at least two hours before the start.

Energy and Carbo-loading Drinks

Sports or energy drinks are a blend of carbohydrates (sucrose, dextrose) and electrolytes; the latter are important to the body in that they help with the absorption of fluids and to transport ions through the bloodstream. It helps to take on carbohydrates in the form of these drinks during a race or heavy training, as they are easily absorbed into the bloodstream and help runners to keep going by saving the muscles' precious glycogen stores.

The specialist carbo-loading sports drink differs from the above in that up to one-fifth of the solution consists of long-chain-molecule (and therefore slow-release) carbohydrates consisting of corn sugar. Where the energy drink has a 6—8 per cent carbohydrate concentration, the carbo-loading type has a 90 per cent concentration. Both types generally contain sodium (salt), potassium, magnesium, zinc and vitamin C, and in terms of sugars, maltodextrin (long-chain, slow-release), fructose (short-chain, slow-release), dextrose or glucose, and sucrose (short-chain, quick release).

During a three-day carbo-loading session, it is good practice to ingest 1—1.5 litres of a special carbo-load drink every day as part of your daily diet. This both contributes to glycogen storage and keeps up your important fluid intake. It is important to drink lots of water during the three days. The carbohydrates from these drinks are good for helping runners to break through the 'wall' which could occur during the course of the race.

Runners should be aware that their weight will increase during the carbo-loading process, since every gram of additional carbohydrate is accompanied by double that amount in water. A runner could put on up to 2kg (4½ lb).

BELOW *There is an enormous range of products on the market to support athletes in their efforts to provide their bodies with energy and prevent dehydration. Besides water and fruit juices, many products — such as sports drinks and carbo-loading formulas — have been scientifically devised to supply distance runners with the correct balance of carbohydrates and electrolytes.*

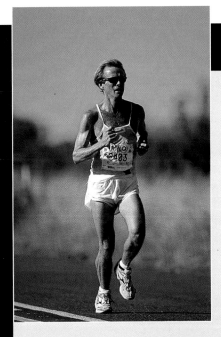

Fordyce's 10 Laws of Training

1 Use Joe Henderson's (*Runner's World USA* columnist) 10-minute test for every run: no matter how tired or sluggish you may feel, give yourself 10 minutes into the jog; if things haven't improved by then, head home.

2 Train to run first for distance; only then train for speed. Once you have achieved your fitness for distance, do specific quality training for speed — for a faster pace in a long-distance race, you need to train to run faster.

3 Never be afraid to take a day off, especially when you're unduly tired, sore or stiff, or have an upper respiratory tract infection. Sometimes rest can be as important as the training itself while preparing for your distance running.

4 Time your training correctly: assuming you have built up a solid base, we now accept that six to eight weeks of intense training is sufficient to produce optimum results.

5 Desperately keen runners must beware the 'plods' — that dead-legged, heavy feeling accompanied by a corresponding mental lack of enthusiasm that is the result of overtraining. The 'superplods' will result if runners respond not by resting and cutting back as they should but by training even harder!

6 Judge your fitness for a very long race by gauging your performance over short distances. Improvement at 5km (3 miles) or 10km (6 miles) is a sure sign that you are ready for good longer race performances.

7 It is important to taper before a major race; it is only when you are well rested and your muscles are fresh that you will race well.

8 On hot days, hydrate early on in the race. Take a bottle of fluid to the start line and drink the contents shortly before the gun goes off.

9 While participating in a race, aim for even-paced running; to do this, start cautiously, conserve your strength, and only later pick up the pace.

10 Don't enter too many marathon races through the year: if you want great results, race selectively and sparingly.

THE ULTRAMARATHON

Ultramarathons encompass a wide range of distances — anything from 50km (31 miles) up to 160km (100 miles), and from 24-hour races to six-day races (these should really be called mega-mileage marathons!). The most commonly raced distance, however, is the 100km (62-mile) event. There are a number of these raced around the world, and some — such as the Nacht-van-Vlaanderen (Belgium) and Winschoten (the Netherlands) — are quite well known. There is also an annual World Championship over 100km; held in different centres each year, teams and individuals from across the globe compete in this event.

Being such extreme events, a number of ultramarathons are held over unusual point-to-point courses or on differing terrain. In the USA, the Western States 100 Miler [160km] is run on the road and paths between Squaw Valley and Sacramento; the Old Dominion 100 Miler is also run as a trail race. The JFK 50 Miler [80km], run on both road and trail, is the USA's oldest ultra. In Europe, the famous Spartathlon is a 250km (155-mile) run in Greece and in South Africa the 56km (35-mile) Two Oceans Marathon and the 90km (56-mile) Comrades Marathon are well known.

Experienced ultramarathoners know that the greatest mistake inexperienced runners make in their approach to ultra-running is to do too much training. They apply incorrect logic, believing that

because ultras are longer than ordinary marathons, the training should also be longer and harder. This is completely wrong and can only lead to injury, illness and frustration.

In fact, there is very little difference in training between an ultramarathon and a standard marathon — both require the same preparation. Inexperienced distance runners are advised to simply train as if they were running an ordinary 42km (26-mile) marathon. It can help to do a handful of longer runs, but it is very important to be cautious.

TRAINING FOR ULTRAS
Long Runs

This is essentially exactly the same as for marathons, however a few longer runs can be added. Extra long runs of up to 70km (43 miles) are useful to build endurance. Beyond this distance, however, running is counterproductive. It simply leaves runners' leg muscles too painful and damaged, and prevents them from training consistently in the following days. Runs should be done very slowly, emphasizing time spent on the legs rather than the speed of the training. Once more, it is important to realize that it is not necessary to run 100km (60 miles) in one session in order to complete that 100km race.

Hillwork

Hillwork can build strength — and it is leg muscle strength that keeps runners going beyond 42km (26 miles). Runners should choose hilly courses on which to train and should also incorporate specific hill training sessions in their weekly training schedules to build the necessary strength. A warm-up run of about 4 to 5 km (2½ to 3 miles) should be followed by between five to 10 sprint repetitions up a steep hill of about 400m (440yd) in length (see p69). Repeated once a week and combined with daily running on hilly courses will produce the strength for ultramarathon running.

Rest

A poorly used and badly understood part of a distance runner's preparation, rest is very important for any runner. For someone contemplating an ultramarathon, it is absolutely vital. Such runners usually taper their training significantly in the weeks leading up to the race and most will hardly train at all in the days immediately prior to the race. Since the race is going to be so long and gruelling, it is best to rest up as much as possible beforehand.

Mental Stamina and Strength

We totally underestimate the power of the mind. When we come to the end of an exhausting 42km (26-mile) marathon, it seems utterly impossible that we could ever tackle an ultramarathon. However, our brain programmes us mentally for being on the road longer; instead of preparing to approach the 30km (18-mile) marker as the halfway mark, the mind will set its sights way past that distance in the longer race. Also, the excitement of a marathon, the crowd support, and the encouragement of fellow runners bring with them a sense of purpose and adventure, all of which pull a runner through. It is a challenge the mind is only too ready to meet.

Successful Comrades ultramarathon participant, Tim Noakes wrote in his book *Lore of Running*: '. . . I find sufficient energy to use the last trick of the ailing runner — a trick learnt from a friend: "Run from face to face. Look into the eyes of each spectator. Look at their joy. Imagine who they are, what they do, how much they want you to do well. Let them pull you through".'

RIGHT *In the end, what is remembered way beyond the muscle bruising and blisters is the charged atmosphere of a marathon together with the camaraderie of thousands of participants running alongside you, sharing your pain.*

Training schedule for an ultramarathon

	Monday	Tuesday	Wednesday	Thursday	Friday	Saturday	Sunday
Week 1	Rest	12–15km (7–9 miles) at steady pace	15–20km (9–12 miles)	Hill session	10km (6 miles)	8km (5 miles)	50km (30 miles) slowly
Week 2	Rest	12–15km (7–9 miles) at steady pace	15–20km (9–12 miles)	Hill session	10km (6 miles)	8km (5 miles)	30km (19 miles) slowly
Week 3	Rest	12–15km (7–9 miles) at steady pace	15–20km (9–12 miles)	Hill session	10km (6 miles)	8km (5 miles)	60km (37 miles) very slowly
Week 4	Rest	8km (5 miles)	10km 6 miles)	Hill session	Rest	8km (5 miles)	18km (11 miles)
Week 5	Rest	10km (6 miles)	5km (3 miles)	Rest	Rest	Rest	RACE

Many runners recommend focusing on the physical processes your body is undergoing — an intense concentration on your breathing, on running efficiently, on maintaining a steady pace. Mental focus is one of the crucial elements of a gruelling race.

Confidence and positive thinking is another. You need to learn to adjust for changing conditions, mishaps, external influences you can't control. In this case, don't focus on the negative; rather modify your game plan to suit the specific situation.

Everyone experiences a bad patch during the marathon when he or she loses rhythm. When this happens to you, slow up on the pace, adjust your stride, and focus on your breathing. Don't push yourself. You can usually recover if you do so. What is important is to concentrate on keeping moving forward; if you stop, your muscles could seize and prevent you from continuing.

In the end, training and willpower are what take over when you start tiring in a long race. Alberto Salazar once said: 'The marathon is slow enough that anyone can stay with you if he wants, if he has the will. The marathon is ultimately a test of will.'

MEGA-DISTANCE MARATHONS

These distance races are on the very fringes of the sport of distance running, and it is only the very few who try them. Once again, as with ultramarathons, there is an incorrect school of thought that believes because the distance to be run is extreme, the training must be equally extreme. This is not so. In fact, almost the opposite applies. When speaking to multi-day runner Karina Nequin (USA) a few years ago, she told me that the best way to train for a six-day race was not to train at all! Her comment was slightly tongue-in-cheek, but there is sense in what she implied. If the body is going to be asked to endure many hours, or even days, of running, it is vital to be race-fit but extremely well rested as well.

Pace during the race is particularly important for ultra distances. Don't overdo this during the beginning stages as there are a lot of kilometres to cover if you misjudge your speed and end up with depleted energy reserves halfway through the race.

In addition to training, a lot of attention has to be placed on fluid and food intake. Easily digestible, light meals high in carbohydrates taken at frequent intervals are best. It is a well-known fact, however, that ultra-runners can have very strange cravings while running. Trevor 'Eat Soup' Parry is a good example.

OPPOSITE *Races held in the colder European climates are characterized by runners clad in 'space blankets' after the race to retain body heat.*

RIGHT *South African marathoner extraordinaire, Donovan Wright, embodies here the 'loneliness' of the long distance runner, an experience every marathoner undergoes at some point in his or her running career.*

MEMORABLE DISTANCE RUNNERS

THE SCENE IS BURNT INTO THE MEMORY OF ALL WHO SAW IT IN 1960 — THE GAUNT AND BAREFOOT ABEBE BIKILA STRIDING ALONG ROME'S TORCHLIT VIA APPIA.

Dorando Pietri (ITALY)

The 1908 Olympic Marathon in London was officially won by Johnny (John Joseph) Hayes of the USA but the most famous runner — and the greatest 'winner' — of that race was Italian Dorando Pietri. In hot, humid conditions he had relentlessly caught up with and passed the leading runner a mile outside the stadium. Exhausted and dehydrated, Pietri fell several times before 100,000 anxious and screaming spectators; each time he was helped to his feet by willing officials. He collapsed across the line, and was carried away on a stretcher. Naturally disqualified (having broken the policy of running unassisted), Queen Alexandra honoured Pietri the next day in the stadium with a golden replica of the trophy awarded to Hayes.

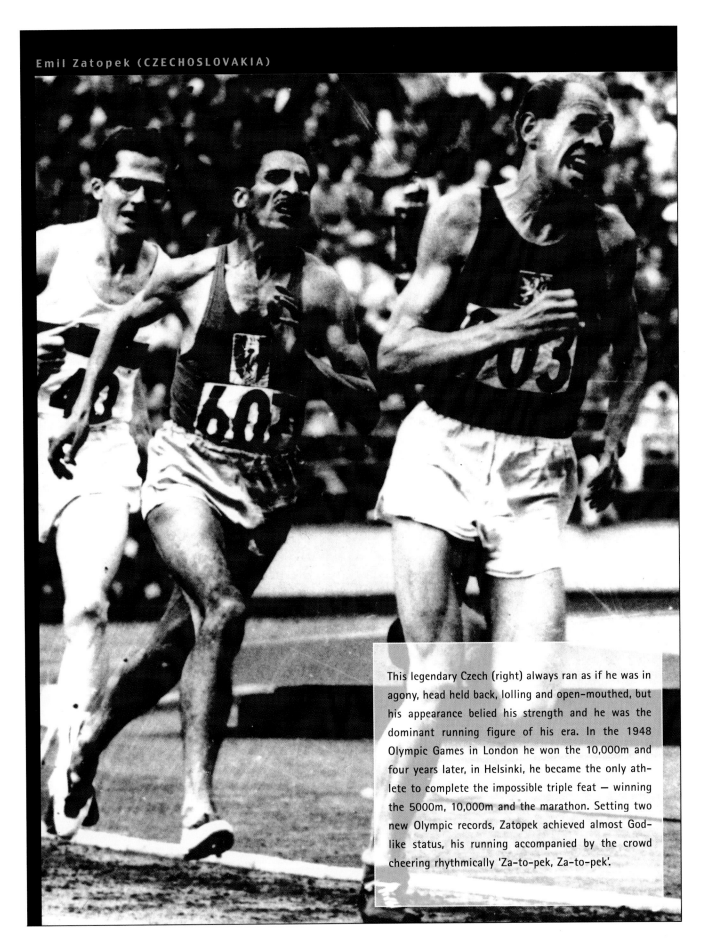

This legendary Czech (right) always ran as if he was in agony, head held back, lolling and open-mouthed, but his appearance belied his strength and he was the dominant running figure of his era. In the 1948 Olympic Games in London he won the 10,000m and four years later, in Helsinki, he became the only athlete to complete the impossible triple feat — winning the 5000m, 10,000m and the marathon. Setting two new Olympic records, Zatopek achieved almost God-like status, his running accompanied by the crowd cheering rhythmically 'Za-to-pek, Za-to-pek'.

Clarence de Mar (USA)

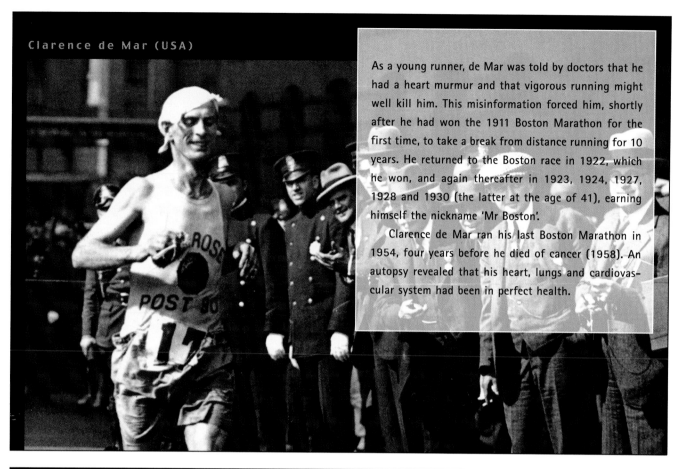

As a young runner, de Mar was told by doctors that he had a heart murmur and that vigorous running might well kill him. This misinformation forced him, shortly after he had won the 1911 Boston Marathon for the first time, to take a break from distance running for 10 years. He returned to the Boston race in 1922, which he won, and again thereafter in 1923, 1924, 1927, 1928 and 1930 (the latter at the age of 41), earning himself the nickname 'Mr Boston'.

Clarence de Mar ran his last Boston Marathon in 1954, four years before he died of cancer (1958). An autopsy revealed that his heart, lungs and cardiovascular system had been in perfect health.

Grete Waitz (NORWAY)

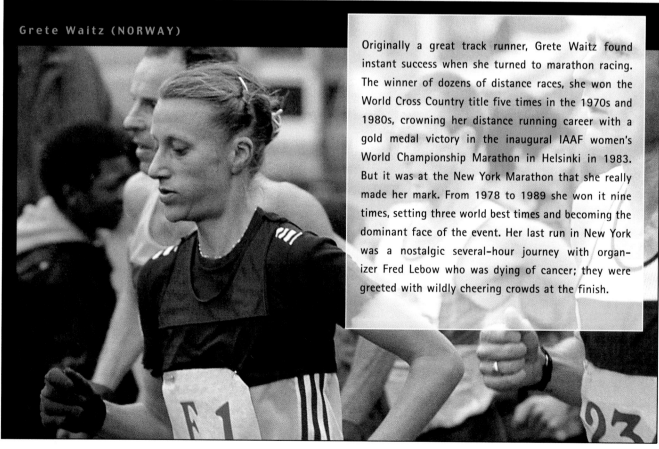

Originally a great track runner, Grete Waitz found instant success when she turned to marathon racing. The winner of dozens of distance races, she won the World Cross Country title five times in the 1970s and 1980s, crowning her distance running career with a gold medal victory in the inaugural IAAF women's World Championship Marathon in Helsinki in 1983. But it was at the New York Marathon that she really made her mark. From 1978 to 1989 she won it nine times, setting three world best times and becoming the dominant face of the event. Her last run in New York was a nostalgic several-hour journey with organizer Fred Lebow who was dying of cancer; they were greeted with wildly cheering crowds at the finish.

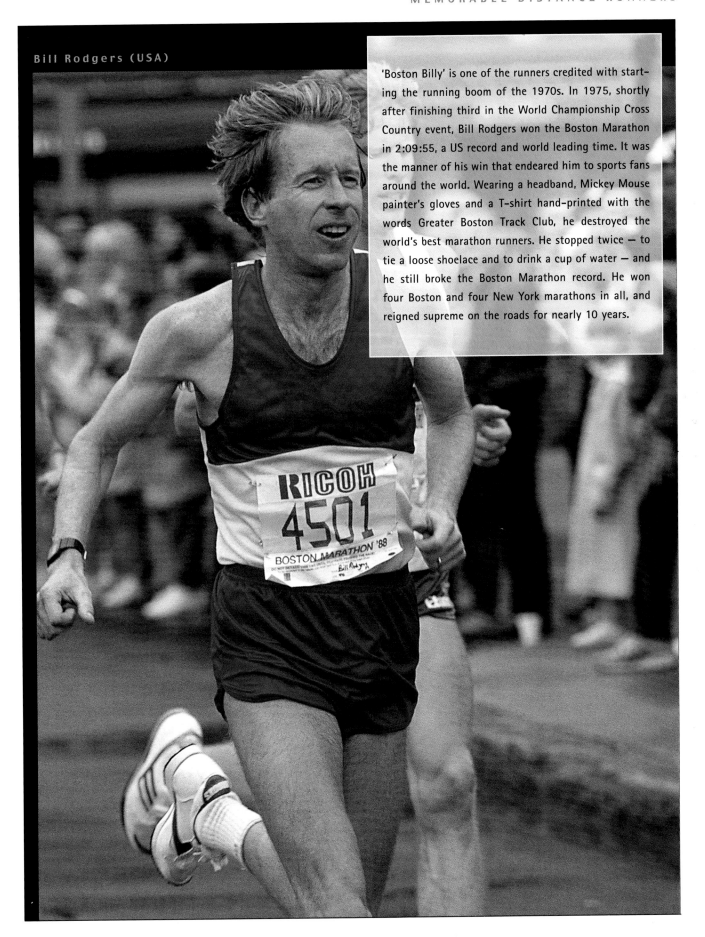

Bill Rodgers (USA)

'Boston Billy' is one of the runners credited with start-ing the running boom of the 1970s. In 1975, shortly after finishing third in the World Championship Cross Country event, Bill Rodgers won the Boston Marathon in 2:09:55, a US record and world leading time. It was the manner of his win that endeared him to sports fans around the world. Wearing a headband, Mickey Mouse painter's gloves and a T-shirt hand-printed with the words Greater Boston Track Club, he destroyed the world's best marathon runners. He stopped twice — to tie a loose shoelace and to drink a cup of water — and he still broke the Boston Marathon record. He won four Boston and four New York marathons in all, and reigned supreme on the roads for nearly 10 years.

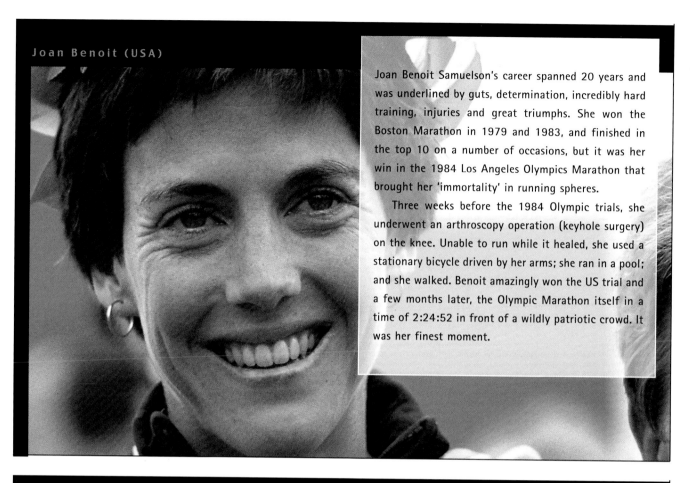

Joan Benoit (USA)

Joan Benoit Samuelson's career spanned 20 years and was underlined by guts, determination, incredibly hard training, injuries and great triumphs. She won the Boston Marathon in 1979 and 1983, and finished in the top 10 on a number of occasions, but it was her win in the 1984 Los Angeles Olympics Marathon that brought her 'immortality' in running spheres.

Three weeks before the 1984 Olympic trials, she underwent an arthroscopy operation (keyhole surgery) on the knee. Unable to run while it healed, she used a stationary bicycle driven by her arms; she ran in a pool; and she walked. Benoit amazingly won the US trial and a few months later, the Olympic Marathon itself in a time of 2:24:52 in front of a wildly patriotic crowd. It was her finest moment.

Arthur Newton (GREAT BRITAIN)

In an era (the early 1900s) when runners barely ran the marathon distance in a week's training runs, Arthur 'Greatheart' Newton would do so in a day. He also virtually wrote the first textbooks on how to train for, and race, long distances.

In his career, Newton won five Comrades Marathons, set a record for the London-to-Brighton, and broke the 100 Mile world record a number of times. In March 1928, he ran in the Transcontinental Race, from Los Angeles on the Pacific Ocean to New York on the Atlantic — split into lengths of between 48 and 120km (30 and 75 miles) at a time. He is revered today as the 'father' of distance running.

Frank Shorter (USA)

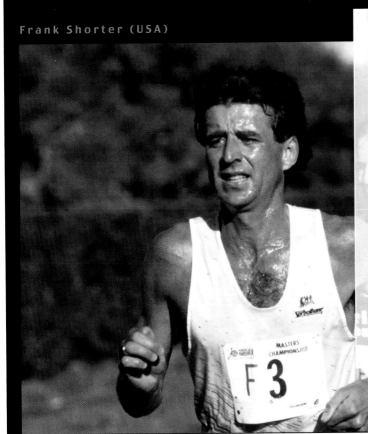

A Yale University law graduate, Frank Shorter, together with Bill Rodgers, is given the honour of contributing to the distance running boom of the 1970s. Shorter's great moment came in the 1972 Olympic Marathon in München. The American team had experienced a bad Olympic Games by their own standards, and the marathon was not an event usually associated with American successes. But Shorter used his track speed (earlier he had come fifth in the 10,000m) to break away from the field at 15km (9 miles). He won by a large margin and his race was beautifully and eloquently described by Erich Segal (author of the famous book *Love Story*). Thousands of television viewers listening to Segal's commentary started running soon after Shorter's victory. In 1976 he went on to win a silver medal in the Olympic Marathon in Montreal.

Wally Hayward (SOUTH AFRICA)

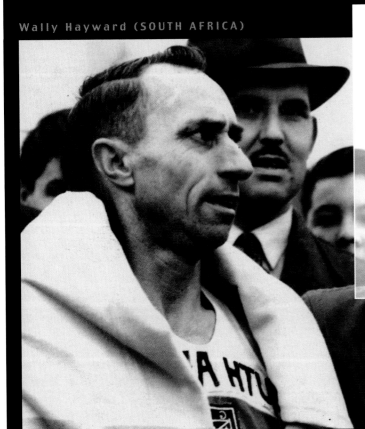

One of the greatest distance runners of all time, Wally Hayward was only 21 when he won his first Comrades Marathon in 1930. Leading by 16 minutes at the halfway mark, he hung on to win by half a minute at the end. He then avoided the Comrades for 20 years, returning in 1950, at 41, to win his second one. Wally went on to repeat this performance in 1951, 1953 and 1954 (at 45), the last two being back-to-back records. In 1988 and 1989 Wally Hayward decided to race the Comrades again at the age of 79 and 80! He ran the 1988 'up route' of the Comrades in nine and three-quarter hours, beating half the field and finishing with an hour and a quarter to spare.

Khalid Khannouchi (MOROCCO)

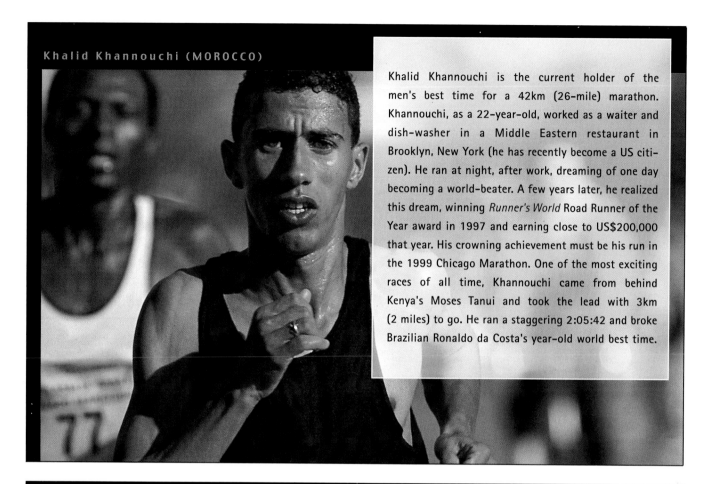

Khalid Khannouchi is the current holder of the men's best time for a 42km (26-mile) marathon. Khannouchi, as a 22-year-old, worked as a waiter and dish-washer in a Middle Eastern restaurant in Brooklyn, New York (he has recently become a US citizen). He ran at night, after work, dreaming of one day becoming a world-beater. A few years later, he realized this dream, winning *Runner's World* Road Runner of the Year award in 1997 and earning close to US$200,000 that year. His crowning achievement must be his run in the 1999 Chicago Marathon. One of the most exciting races of all time, Khannouchi came from behind Kenya's Moses Tanui and took the lead with 3km (2 miles) to go. He ran a staggering 2:05:42 and broke Brazilian Ronaldo da Costa's year-old world best time.

Robert de Castella (AUSTRALIA)

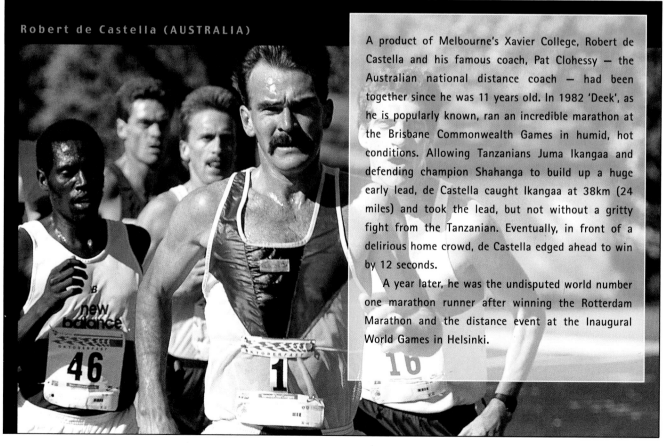

A product of Melbourne's Xavier College, Robert de Castella and his famous coach, Pat Clohessy — the Australian national distance coach — had been together since he was 11 years old. In 1982 'Deek', as he is popularly known, ran an incredible marathon at the Brisbane Commonwealth Games in humid, hot conditions. Allowing Tanzanians Juma Ikangaa and defending champion Shahanga to build up a huge early lead, de Castella caught Ikangaa at 38km (24 miles) and took the lead, but not without a gritty fight from the Tanzanian. Eventually, in front of a delirious home crowd, de Castella edged ahead to win by 12 seconds.

A year later, he was the undisputed world number one marathon runner after winning the Rotterdam Marathon and the distance event at the Inaugural World Games in Helsinki.

Kipchoge Keino (KENYA)

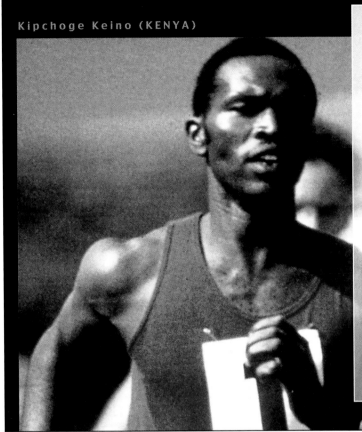

One of the most famous runners of all time, Kip Hezekiah Keino's running was graceful and fast like the gazelles that run across the Kenyan savannah. In the 1968 Olympic Games at Mexico City, the indefatiguable Keino competed in the 1500m, 5000m and 10,000m. Counting heats and finals, he ran six world-class races in eight days. Keino lost the 5000m by a whisker to Tunisia's Mohamed Gammoudi, and won the 1500m final by the biggest winning margin in Olympic 1500m history — in the process defeating the USA's brilliant star, Jim Ryun. The race was a wonderful example of Kenyan teamwork: teammate Ben Jipcho set a fast pace of 400m in 56 seconds, which helped Keino to break away from Ryun and establish an unassailable lead. Probably one of the greatest 1500m races of all time, it should also be placed in the context of Keino's incredible race schedule prior to the 1500m final.

Ron Hill (GREAT BRITAIN)

One of the 'iron men' of distance running, Ron Hill, a chemistry PhD, is also recognized as a pioneering scientist of the marathon. He took part in three Olympic Games: Tokyo (1964), Mexico (1968) and München (1972), but his greatest marathon victories were the 1969 European Championships, the 1970 Boston Marathon, and the 1970 Commonwealth Games in Edinburgh (his time of 2:09:28 in the latter was the world's second fastest marathon at the time).

Perhaps his greatest contribution, however, lay in his scientific approach to distance running. Dr Ron Hill experimented with different lightweight fabrics and materials for running clothing and shoes. He also popularized a special depletion/carbohydrate-loading diet for runners known as the Saltin diet, believing that it had enabled him to dominate marathon running for those years that he did.

Alberto Salazar (CUBA/USA)

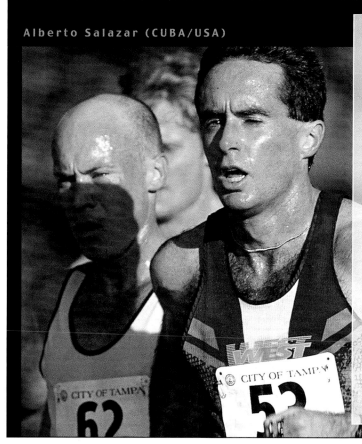

Coached by the famous Bill Dellinger, Alberto Salazar had a reputation as a ferocious competitor but one who sometimes ran himself into the ground to the detriment of his health. Winner of many distance titles including cross country, he collapsed at the famous Falmouth Road Race (12km; 7 miles) in 1978 when, as a relatively young runner, he chased the great Bill Rodgers until the last mile. He was placed in a tub of iced water while a Catholic priest administered the last rites! He was also hospitalized after his wins in the 1982 Boston and 1994 Comrades marathons.

After dethroning four-time New York Marathon winner Bill Rodgers in the 1980 race, Alberto Salazar won New York again in 1981 and then dominated 1982 with a second place in the World Cross Country Championships and a thrilling two-second win over American Dick Beardsley in Boston. Thereafter, Salazar's career went into decline, with injuries and illness being the result of a shattered immune system.

Abebe Bikila (KENYA)

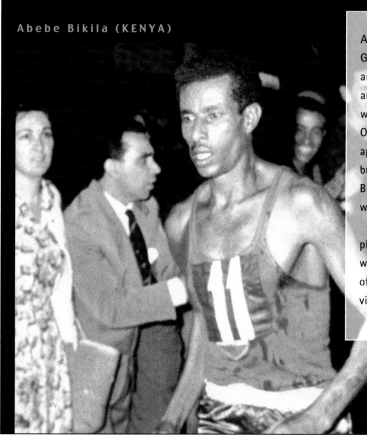

Abebe Bikila's marathon victory in the 1960 Olympic Games in Rome, Italy, was a triumph for his country and an inspiration to the whole continent of Africa — an unknown black man had defeated the best of the world's long distance runners. Then in the Tokyo Olympic Games in 1964, Abebe Bikila had had an appendectomy six weeks prior to the marathon race, but despite the setback he felt he was ready to race. Bikila won gold in the Olympic Marathon, setting a world record at the same time.

In 1969, when a car accident left him almost completely paralyzed, he said in an interview, 'It was the will of God that I won the Olympics, and it was the will of God that I met with my accident. I accepted those victories as I accept this tragedy.'

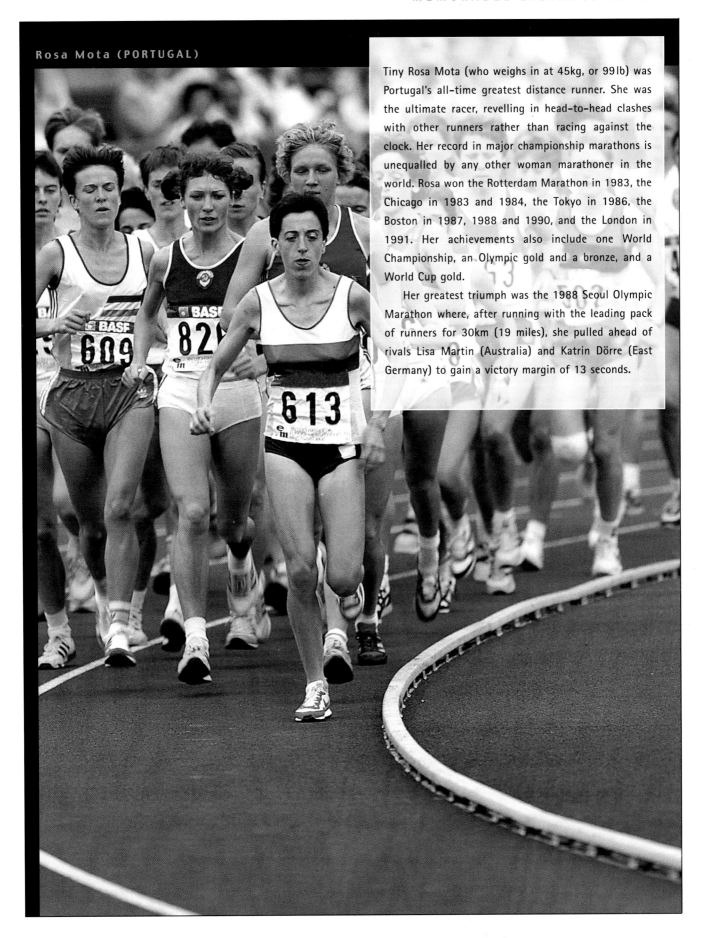

Rosa Mota (PORTUGAL)

Tiny Rosa Mota (who weighs in at 45kg, or 99lb) was Portugal's all-time greatest distance runner. She was the ultimate racer, revelling in head-to-head clashes with other runners rather than racing against the clock. Her record in major championship marathons is unequalled by any other woman marathoner in the world. Rosa won the Rotterdam Marathon in 1983, the Chicago in 1983 and 1984, the Tokyo in 1986, the Boston in 1987, 1988 and 1990, and the London in 1991. Her achievements also include one World Championship, an Olympic gold and a bronze, and a World Cup gold.

Her greatest triumph was the 1988 Seoul Olympic Marathon where, after running with the leading pack of runners for 30km (19 miles), she pulled ahead of rivals Lisa Martin (Australia) and Katrin Dörre (East Germany) to gain a victory margin of 13 seconds.

GREAT WORLD
MARATHONS

IT IS THE CHARISMA AND EXCITEMENT OF A MARATHON, THE CROWD SUPPORT AND THE
ENCOURAGEMENT FROM FELLOW RUNNERS THAT CARRIES A RUNNER THROUGH THE RACE.

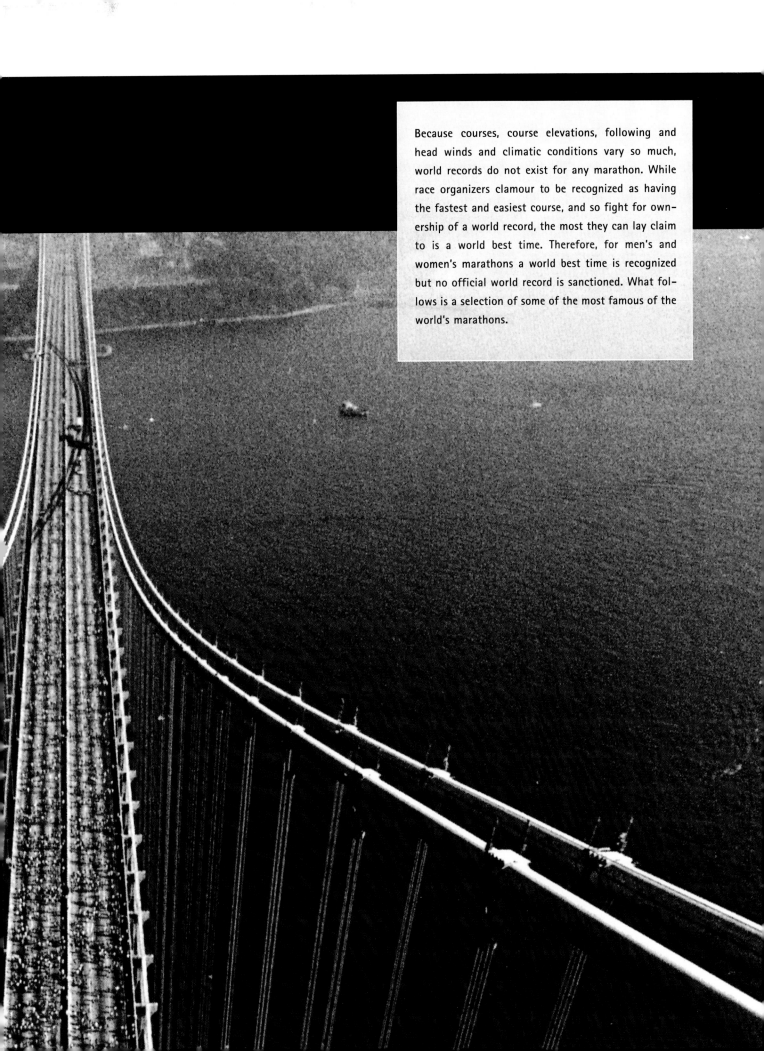

Because courses, course elevations, following and head winds and climatic conditions vary so much, world records do not exist for any marathon. While race organizers clamour to be recognized as having the fastest and easiest course, and so fight for ownership of a world record, the most they can lay claim to is a world best time. Therefore, for men's and women's marathons a world best time is recognized but no official world record is sanctioned. What follows is a selection of some of the most famous of the world's marathons.

ROTTERDAM, NETHERLANDS

This has become the Netherlands' most famous marathon. Extremely well organized, it is known for its very fast, flat course over which a number of thrilling marathons have been run — and a number of world best times recorded. Organized by Jos Hermans, himself a former distance world record-holder and Olympian, the race is held on the same weekend as the London Marathon.

Among famous racers at Rotterdam were Alberto Salazar (USA) and Robert de Castella (Australia), who engaged in a titanic clash in 1983 (de Castella won in 2:08:37). Carlos Lopes of Portugal was another; a few weeks shy of his fortieth birthday in 1985, he set an incredible, paced world record of 2:07:11 the same year Welshman Steve Jones ran 2:07:12 at the Chicago Marathon in October.

Lopes's record was broken by Belayneh Dinsamo of Ethiopia in 1988. Behind Dinsamo, Ahmed Salah of Djibouti was the next marathoner to break the world best time — but not as a winner (Dinsamo's time was 2:06:50, Salah's 2:07:07).

Recently Tegla Laroupes's best women's time — a shade over 2:20 — has underlined the course's reputation as a fast one.

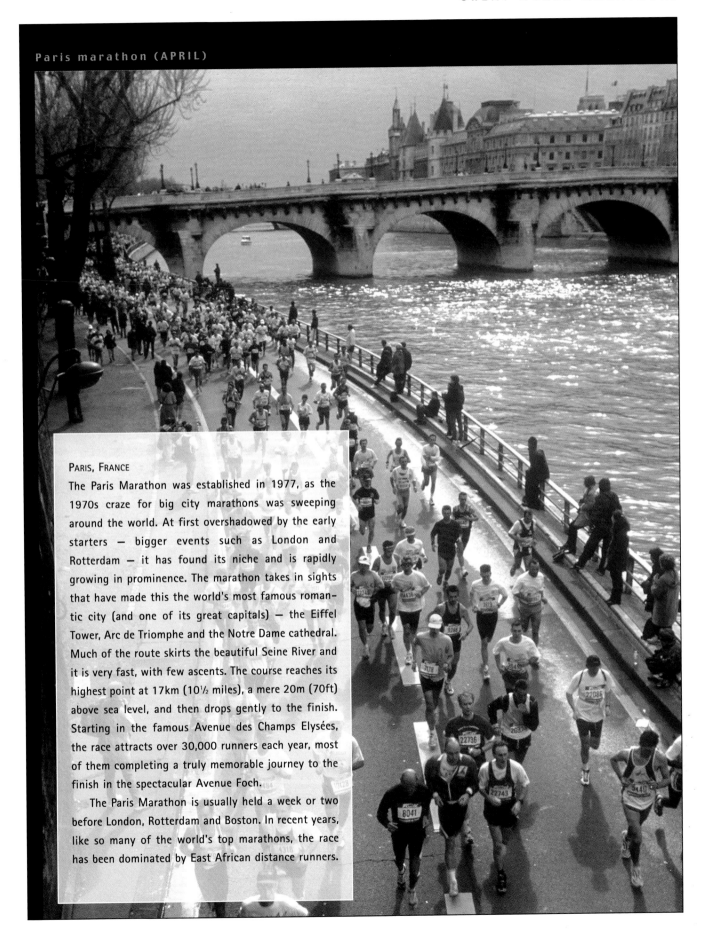

Paris marathon (APRIL)

PARIS, FRANCE

The Paris Marathon was established in 1977, as the 1970s craze for big city marathons was sweeping around the world. At first overshadowed by the early starters — bigger events such as London and Rotterdam — it has found its niche and is rapidly growing in prominence. The marathon takes in sights that have made this the world's most famous romantic city (and one of its great capitals) — the Eiffel Tower, Arc de Triomphe and the Notre Dame cathedral. Much of the route skirts the beautiful Seine River and it is very fast, with few ascents. The course reaches its highest point at 17km (10½ miles), a mere 20m (70ft) above sea level, and then drops gently to the finish. Starting in the famous Avenue des Champs Elysées, the race attracts over 30,000 runners each year, most of them completing a truly memorable journey to the finish in the spectacular Avenue Foch.

The Paris Marathon is usually held a week or two before London, Rotterdam and Boston. In recent years, like so many of the world's top marathons, the race has been dominated by East African distance runners.

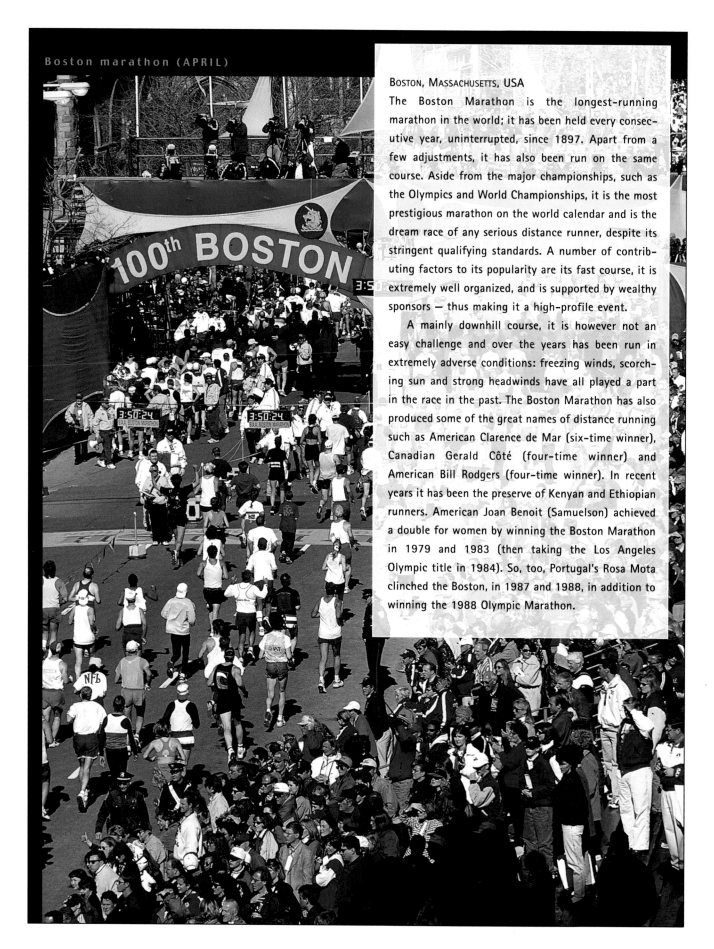

100th BOSTON

3:50:24 B.A.A. BOSTON MARATHON

3:50:24 B.A.A. BOSTON MARATHON

BOSTON, MASSACHUSETTS, USA

The Boston Marathon is the longest-running marathon in the world; it has been held every consecutive year, uninterrupted, since 1897. Apart from a few adjustments, it has also been run on the same course. Aside from the major championships, such as the Olympics and World Championships, it is the most prestigious marathon on the world calendar and is the dream race of any serious distance runner, despite its stringent qualifying standards. A number of contributing factors to its popularity are its fast course, it is extremely well organized, and is supported by wealthy sponsors — thus making it a high-profile event.

A mainly downhill course, it is however not an easy challenge and over the years has been run in extremely adverse conditions: freezing winds, scorching sun and strong headwinds have all played a part in the race in the past. The Boston Marathon has also produced some of the great names of distance running such as American Clarence de Mar (six-time winner), Canadian Gerald Côté (four-time winner) and American Bill Rodgers (four-time winner). In recent years it has been the preserve of Kenyan and Ethiopian runners. American Joan Benoit (Samuelson) achieved a double for women by winning the Boston Marathon in 1979 and 1983 (then taking the Los Angeles Olympic title in 1984). So, too, Portugal's Rosa Mota clinched the Boston, in 1987 and 1988, in addition to winning the 1988 Olympic Marathon.

London marathon (APRIL)

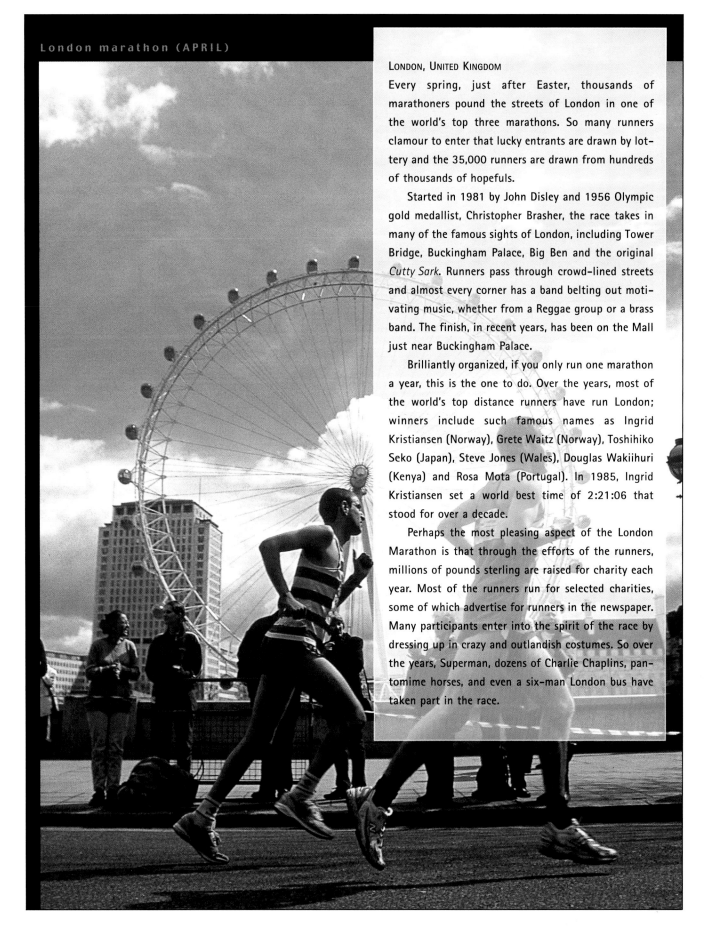

LONDON, UNITED KINGDOM

Every spring, just after Easter, thousands of marathoners pound the streets of London in one of the world's top three marathons. So many runners clamour to enter that lucky entrants are drawn by lottery and the 35,000 runners are drawn from hundreds of thousands of hopefuls.

Started in 1981 by John Disley and 1956 Olympic gold medallist, Christopher Brasher, the race takes in many of the famous sights of London, including Tower Bridge, Buckingham Palace, Big Ben and the original *Cutty Sark*. Runners pass through crowd-lined streets and almost every corner has a band belting out motivating music, whether from a Reggae group or a brass band. The finish, in recent years, has been on the Mall just near Buckingham Palace.

Brilliantly organized, if you only run one marathon a year, this is the one to do. Over the years, most of the world's top distance runners have run London; winners include such famous names as Ingrid Kristiansen (Norway), Grete Waitz (Norway), Toshihiko Seko (Japan), Steve Jones (Wales), Douglas Wakiihuri (Kenya) and Rosa Mota (Portugal). In 1985, Ingrid Kristiansen set a world best time of 2:21:06 that stood for over a decade.

Perhaps the most pleasing aspect of the London Marathon is that through the efforts of the runners, millions of pounds sterling are raised for charity each year. Most of the runners run for selected charities, some of which advertise for runners in the newspaper. Many participants enter into the spirit of the race by dressing up in crazy and outlandish costumes. So over the years, Superman, dozens of Charlie Chaplins, pantomime horses, and even a six-man London bus have taken part in the race.

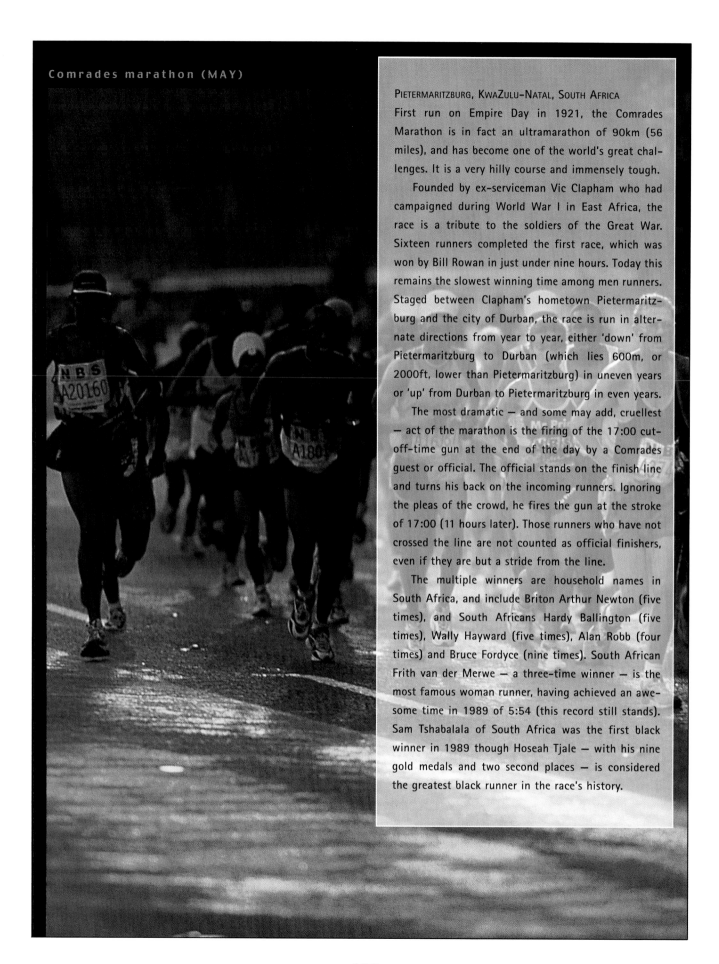

Pietermaritzburg, KwaZulu-Natal, South Africa

First run on Empire Day in 1921, the Comrades Marathon is in fact an ultramarathon of 90km (56 miles), and has become one of the world's great challenges. It is a very hilly course and immensely tough.

Founded by ex-serviceman Vic Clapham who had campaigned during World War I in East Africa, the race is a tribute to the soldiers of the Great War. Sixteen runners completed the first race, which was won by Bill Rowan in just under nine hours. Today this remains the slowest winning time among men runners. Staged between Clapham's hometown Pietermaritzburg and the city of Durban, the race is run in alternate directions from year to year, either 'down' from Pietermaritzburg to Durban (which lies 600m, or 2000ft, lower than Pietermaritzburg) in uneven years or 'up' from Durban to Pietermaritzburg in even years.

The most dramatic — and some may add, cruellest — act of the marathon is the firing of the 17:00 cut-off-time gun at the end of the day by a Comrades guest or official. The official stands on the finish line and turns his back on the incoming runners. Ignoring the pleas of the crowd, he fires the gun at the stroke of 17:00 (11 hours later). Those runners who have not crossed the line are not counted as official finishers, even if they are but a stride from the line.

The multiple winners are household names in South Africa, and include Briton Arthur Newton (five times), and South Africans Hardy Ballington (five times), Wally Hayward (five times), Alan Robb (four times) and Bruce Fordyce (nine times). South African Frith van der Merwe — a three-time winner — is the most famous woman runner, having achieved an awesome time in 1989 of 5:54 (this record still stands). Sam Tshabalala of South Africa was the first black winner in 1989 though Hoseah Tjale — with his nine gold medals and two second places — is considered the greatest black runner in the race's history.

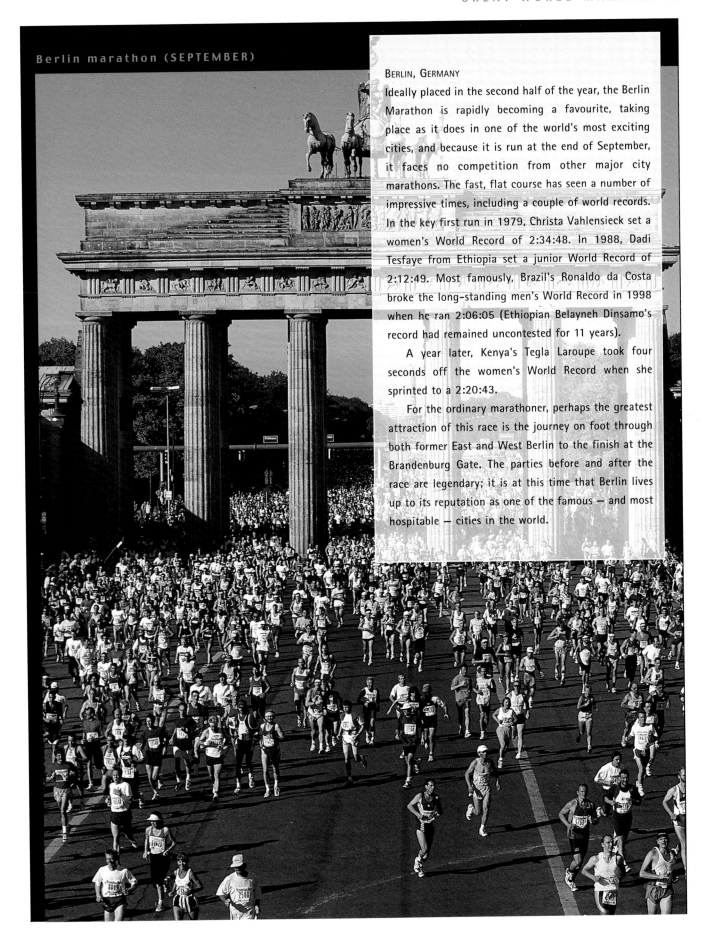

Berlin marathon (SEPTEMBER)

BERLIN, GERMANY

Ideally placed in the second half of the year, the Berlin Marathon is rapidly becoming a favourite, taking place as it does in one of the world's most exciting cities, and because it is run at the end of September, it faces no competition from other major city marathons. The fast, flat course has seen a number of impressive times, including a couple of world records. In the key first run in 1979, Christa Vahlensieck set a women's World Record of 2:34:48. In 1988, Dadi Tesfaye from Ethiopia set a junior World Record of 2:12:49. Most famously, Brazil's Ronaldo da Costa broke the long-standing men's World Record in 1998 when he ran 2:06:05 (Ethiopian Belayneh Dinsamo's record had remained uncontested for 11 years).

A year later, Kenya's Tegla Laroupe took four seconds off the women's World Record when she sprinted to a 2:20:43.

For the ordinary marathoner, perhaps the greatest attraction of this race is the journey on foot through both former East and West Berlin to the finish at the Brandenburg Gate. The parties before and after the race are legendary; it is at this time that Berlin lives up to its reputation as one of the famous — and most hospitable — cities in the world.

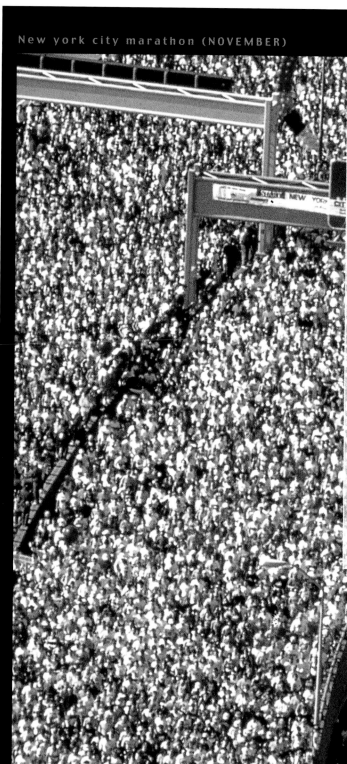

NEW YORK, NEW YORK, USA

Originally a small marathon championship race held within the bounds of the Big Apple's famous Central Park, this is now the world's biggest marathon among male participants, alongside the London Marathon. Every year close on 40,000 runners make the journey through New York's five boroughs. From Staten Island, marathoners cross the vast Verrazano Narrows bridge to run along crowd-lined streets through Brooklyn, Queens, the Bronx, and Manhattan, ending in Central Park. The race crosses a number of major bridges (including the famous Brooklyn Bridge) and takes in most of New York City's famous sites.

From its humble beginnings, chief organizer Fred Lebow's tireless efforts to promote it paid off when he persuaded the City Fathers and New Yorkers in general to take the race seriously, to move it beyond the boundaries of Central Park, and finally, when charismatic Bill Rodgers won it four times in succession from 1976, his wonderfully run races drew enormous attention to the event. Bitterly disappointed by his poor run in the 1976 Montreal Olympics, Rodgers came to the New York Marathon determined to make an impact. His head-to-head clash with Frank Shorter (the 1972 Olympics Marathon champion) and winning time of 2:10 instantly put the race on the map.

Fukuoka marathon (DECEMBER)

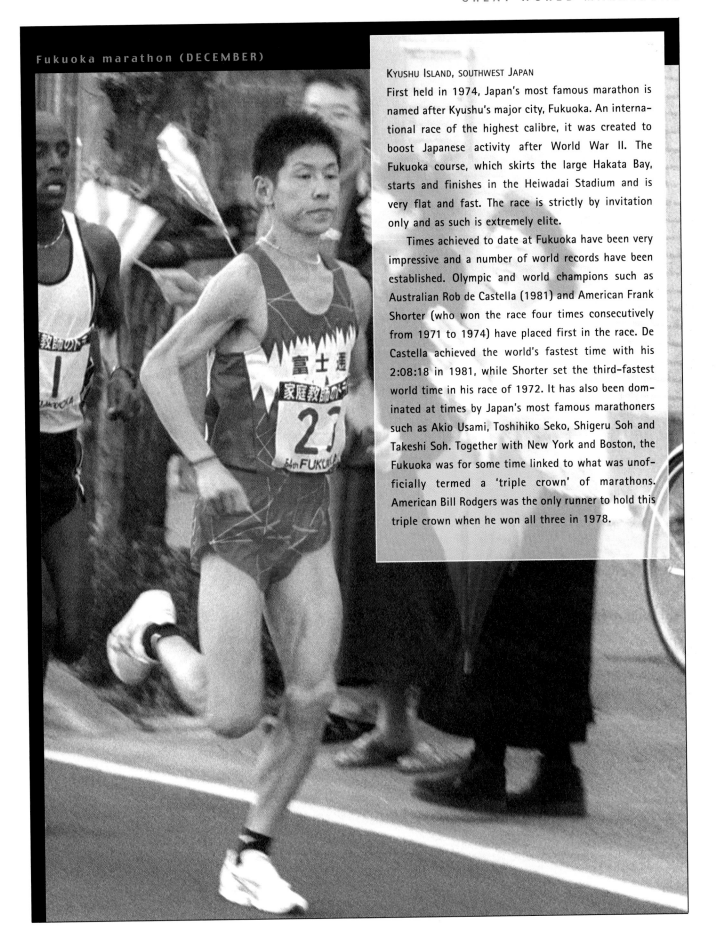

KYUSHU ISLAND, SOUTHWEST JAPAN

First held in 1974, Japan's most famous marathon is named after Kyushu's major city, Fukuoka. An international race of the highest calibre, it was created to boost Japanese activity after World War II. The Fukuoka course, which skirts the large Hakata Bay, starts and finishes in the Heiwadai Stadium and is very flat and fast. The race is strictly by invitation only and as such is extremely elite.

Times achieved to date at Fukuoka have been very impressive and a number of world records have been established. Olympic and world champions such as Australian Rob de Castella (1981) and American Frank Shorter (who won the race four times consecutively from 1971 to 1974) have placed first in the race. De Castella achieved the world's fastest time with his 2:08:18 in 1981, while Shorter set the third-fastest world time in his race of 1972. It has also been dominated at times by Japan's most famous marathoners such as Akio Usami, Toshihiko Seko, Shigeru Soh and Takeshi Soh. Together with New York and Boston, the Fukuoka was for some time linked to what was unofficially termed a 'triple crown' of marathons. American Bill Rodgers was the only runner to hold this triple crown when he won all three in 1978.

ACKNOWLEDGEMENTS

BRUCE FORDYCE

I would like to thank Mariëlle Renssen, especially, for her tireless efforts in the marathon task of producing this book. In reality, the authorship should read: Mariëlle Renssen with Bruce Fordyce — and not vice versa.

Thanks to Renée Scott, marathoner extraordinaire, who placed eighth overall in the 2001 Comrades Marathon to win her first Comrades gold medal, and who was a stunning model for the stretching photographs. Thanks also to Professor Tim Noakes who perused all the scientific text and whose contribution to distance running over the years has far exceeded that of any single runner anywhere in the world; to Dr Andrew Bosch at the Sports Science Institute; and to Dr Graham Louw from UCT Medical School for checking our anatomical artwork.

MARIËLLE RENSSEN

Special thanks go to Patrick Hill for coaxing me through my first half marathon; also to the runners who gave so willingly of their time for our photo shoot: Ann Easton, Sue Tracey, Kathy McQuaid, Patrick Cox and Glenn Castle, as well as Jayne Nuttall, who flexed her limber muscles in our weightwork section; Logans Sportsman's Warehouse who kindly lent us their equipment for the photo shoots, and photographer Ryno, for his superb studio work and delectable food shots; and to Mark Radnay of Yum, who cooked up a storm for the nutrition section. I'd like to acknowledge the crucial role played by *Runner's World* magazine, which acts as a constant source of valuable information to runners around the globe. Finally, thanks to talented designer Claire van Rhyn who has worked magic with her creative skills.

CONSULTANTS

BRUCE TULLOH

British-born Bruce Tulloh was one of Great Britain's most successful distance runners in the 1960s, representing his country in the 1500—10,000m distances in addition to cross-country and ultradistance running. He won gold in the 5000-metre event at the European Games in 1962 and is the former holder of the 1969 record for the America Transcontinental race from Los Angeles to New York.

Bruce has coached several British international athletes, including Richard Nerurkar — who won the 1993 World Marathon Cup and placed fifth in the Marathon event at the 1996 Olympics in Atlanta, Georgia. Bruce is also the former Coaching Editor of *Runner's World* (UK) and the author of more than a dozen books on running and fitness. He still runs almost daily, and even in his mid-sixties succeeded in breaking three hours for a marathon.

TIM NOAKES

A qualified medical doctor, sports physician and exercise scientist who has focused his career on research into sports science and medicine, South African Tim Noakes has written more than 300 articles for leading scientific publications. He is also the author of *Lore of Running* and co-author of three other sports books. Tim started his long-distance running career in 1972, and with his last marathon in 1990 he had run over 70 long-distance races, including seven Comrades marathons. Today he is the Discovery Health Professor of Exercise and Sports Science at the University of Cape Town (UCT) and Director of the UCT and Medical Research Council Research Unit for Exercise Science and Sports Medicine. He is a fellow of the American College of Sports Medicine, and in 1999, was elected as a founding member of the International Olympic Committee (IOC) Olympic Science Academy.

INDEX

Numbers in bold refer to photographs. Numbers in *italics* refer to panels, diagrams or illustrations

A

Achilles *115*
Achilles tendon 52, 107, **115**
adenosine triposphate
    see ATP
ADP *25*, 84
alcohol **98**
amino acids 25
ancient athletes **8**
Ancient Greek Olympic
    Games **8**
anorexic 82
antioxidants 93
ATP 22, *25*, 84

B

Benoit, Joan **140**
Berlin Marathon **153**
Bikila, Abebe 26, **144**
biomechanics 29, 30, 35, 100,
    104, 113
Boston Marathon 11, **150**
Bowerman, Bill 29
Budd, Zola 26, 47

C

carbohydrate replacement 87
carbohydrates 22, 84, 85, *86*,
    90, 91, 130
    complex *85*
    simple *85*
carbo-loading 86, 130
cardiac strengthening 16
cardiovascular system 16
Castella, Robert de 54, **142**
chafing 38
cholesterol 19
circulatory system *18*
clothing 38
    crop top 38, **39, 40**
    Gore-Tex 38, **40**
    hats **39**
    lightweight shorts 38
    long pants **40**
    running vest 38
    socks 38, **39**
club members 64
Coe, Sebastian 61, 66
Comrades Marathon **152**
conditions 102
    anorexia 103
    haematuria 103

heart attack 103
cool-down 107
Cooper Institute 16
corn syrup 91
course 129
Cram, Steve 66

D

dehydration 53, **102**
diarrhoea 53
diet 82
downhill runners 49

E

East African runners 11, **27**
eating plan 82
electrolytes **131**
eletrolyte imbalance 52
Elliot, Herb 69
encouragement **132**
endorphins 44
energy bars 91
energy drinks 130
enzyme 23
equipment 42
    belt 42
    eyewear 42, *43*
    LED 42
    SPF factor **42**
    sunglasses 42
    torture-tested 127
ethylene vinyl acetate *see* EVA
EVA 29
exhaustion **107**

F

family 78, **80**
fartlek 68
fatigue 129
fats 23, 87
    monounsaturated *88*, 89
    polyunsaturated 87, *88*
    saturated 87
fatty acids 23, *25*, 87
first race 80, *81*
fitness 58, 107
flavonoids 92
footwear 107
Fordyce, Bruce 61
    10 Laws of Training *131*
From Half Marathon to
    Ultramarathon 122—135

fructose 25
Fukuoka Marathon **155**
full marathon 124

G

galactose 24
Gebrselassie, Hailie 29
Getting Started 44—57
glucose 24, 84, 91
glucose syrup 81
glycogen **84, 85, 87, 128**
Great World Marathons
    146—155

H

half marathon 122
Hayward, Wally **141**
HDL 19
health 12
heart disease **19**
heart monitor **60**
heart rate 60
Henderson, Joe 66
high-density lipoproteins
    see HDL
hill running 49
Hill, Ron 87, **143**
hillwork **68**, 133
hitting the wall 78
'hooked' **12**
hunter-gatherers **8**
hypoglycaemic 84

I

iliotibial band friction syndrome
    see ITBS
illness 102
Injuries 100—119
injuries 52
    blisters **55**
    chafing 54
    cramps 52
    massage **52**
    medical staff **52**
    stitch 52
injury 100, 108, **111**,
    107, 119
interval training 67, **108**, 126
Introduction 8—13
inverse stretch reflex 72
Isostar **92**
ITBS 28, 113

J

Johnson, Ben 46

K

Keino, Kipchoge **143**
Khannouchi, Khalid **142**

L

lacing system *31*
lactate 64
lacto-ovo-vegetarian 91
lacto-vegetarian 90
LDL 19, 87
Lewis, Carl 46
lipase 23
Liquori, Marti 11
London Marathon **151**
long distance runner **135**
Long Fast Distance 66—67
long runs 132
Long Slow Distance 66
Lore of Running 56, 133
low-density lipoprotein
    see LDL
LSD *see* Long Slow Distance

M

major shoe brands **29**
maltose 25
Mar, Clarence de 16, **138**
massage 52, 81, 108, **113**
medal **122**
mega-distance marathons 135
Memorable Distance Runners
    136—145
mental stamina 133
Meyer, Elana **122**
minerals 96, *96—97*
Mota, Rosa **145**
motivation 129
muscle cell 22, 23
muscle contraction 24
    concentric 24
    eccentric 24
muscle fibre 23
muscle injuries 118
    acute muscle tear 119
    cramping 118
    delayed muscle soreness 118
    insidious muscle tear 119
    spasms 118
    sprains 118

strains 118
muscle structure *22*
muscular injuries **20**
muscular system *106*

N
nature 12
Nequin, Karina 135
neutral foot strike 28, 36
New York City Marathon **125**, **154**
Newton, Arthur **140**
Noakes, Tim 56, 62, 133
nutrition **82**, **103**
Nutrition and Diet 82–99

O
orthotics 28, *32*, **35**
oxygen 23

P
pace **104**
pacing *63*
Paris Marathon **149**
Parry, Trevor 'Eat Soup' 84, 135
performance 66
Pheidippides 8
Philippides *see* Pheidippides
phosphate 25
Physiology 16–25
physiology of running 22
physiotherapists 108
Pietri, Dorando **136**
pit-stop 56, 81
plantar fasciitis 28
pre-race day 127
pronation 26, 28, 36
protein **84**, **89**
psychological 21
pulse rate 60

R
race number **120**
race time *128*
racing shoes 31
rehydration 102
REM sleep 60
rest 133
road-running 108
Robb, Alan 49
Rodgers, Bill 49, 64, 69, **139**
Rotterdam Marathon **148**

runner's diary **50**
runner's high 44
'runner's trots' 56
running (early stages) **47**
running club 57
running economy 64
Running Gear 26–43
running injuries *109*
  Achilles tendonitis 114, 117
  bone injuries 109
  bone stress fractures 110
  chondromalacia patella *112*
  ITBS 113, *114*
  knee-related injuries 111
  ligament and tendon
    injuries 111
  patellar tendonitis 112
  plantar fasciitis 116, 117
  shin splints 109
  tarsal tunnel syndrome 117
running programme **44**
running safely *100*
running shoe 28, 31, *32–33*
running slang *79*
  hitting the wall 79
  bus 79
  aid station/watering table
    79
  bailing 79
  blow 79
  carbo-loading 79
  DNF 79
  PB 79
  seconds/pacers 79
  splits 79
running style 44, *46*

S
Salazar, Alberto 47, 135, **144**
salt **98**
Saltin Depletion Diet 86
Seko, Toshihiko 39
shoe jargon 34
  air 35
  customizing 37
  flexibility 37
  gel 35
  heel counter 34
  heel wedge 37
  last 34
  midsole 35
  orthotics 35

outer sole 35
polyurethane 35
toe box 35
shoes **26**
short distances 64
Shorter, Frank 12, 61, 62, 124, **141**
skeletal system *105*
Smead, Chuck 49
'space blankets' 135
speed endurance 67
speed session **108**
speedplay *see* fartlek
'splits' 51
Sports Science Institute
  (Cape Town) 11
sprinting 23
Squires, Bill 69
stamina **129**
stretches *72–75*
  Achilles tendon 73
  bent-knee sit-ups 75
  calf muscles 73
  calf stretch 73
  hamstring stretch 75
  horizontal stretch 74
  leg stretch 73
  quadriceps 72
  vertical crossed-calf
    stretch 74
stretching *54*, 72
  joints 72
supination 28
supinators 26, 36
supplementation 92, **93**
  competition 92
  training 92

T
talk test 48
technique 44, 49
Thugwane, Josia 68
timing 47
training 61, 64, 69, 104, 108
  cross-training 70
  cycling **70**, 71
  gymwork 71
  sand dunes 69
  snow-shoeing **70**
  swimming 70, 71
  treadmill 70
  walking 71

training build-up *104*
training diary 50
training partner 48, 57
training schedule, beginner's *69*
training schedule, half
  marathon *124*
training sessions 107, 126
training shoes 30
Treacy, John 39
triglycerides 23

U
ultramarathon 132
  Comrades 132
  JFK 50 Miler 132
  Nacht-van-Vlaanderen 132
  Old Dominion 100 Miler
    132
  Spartathlon 132
  Two Oceans **126**, 132
  Western States 100 Miler
    132
  Winschoten 132
uphill running 49

V
Vaseline 55, 81
vegans 90
vegetarian diet 90
visualization 129
vitamins 94, *94–95*
VO$_2$ max 61, *62*

W
Waitz, Grete **138**
water sachets **58**
weight loss 58, 61
weight-lifting 54
weightwork *76*
  calves 76
  hamstrings 76, 77
  quadriceps 76, 77
wellbeing 16
women runners 57

Y
Yifter, Miruts 11
Yoga 54
Your First 10K Race 58–81

Z
Zatopek, Emil **137**

PICTURE CREDITS

COVER			45		RW	88–89		NHIL/R	136	b	EP
(front)	t	NHIL/R	46		SP	90		NHIL/R	137		AS
(main image)		TDF	47		TDF	91		NHIL/R	138	t	CI
(back)		TDF	48		TDF	92		SP	138	b	VS/PR
ENDPAPERS		TDF	49		NHIL/R	93		NHIL/R	139		VS/PR
1		PR/AL	50	t	NHIL/R	94–95		NHIL/R	140	t	VS/PR
2–3	t & b	TDF	50	b	SP	96–97		NHIL/R	140	b	CMA
4–5		INPRA	51		NHIL/R	98	l	NHIL/R	141	t	VS/PR
6–7		AS/MP	52		SB/AI	98–99		TDF	141	b	INPRA
8	t	AKG/JH	53		NHIL/R	100		SB/AI	142	t & b	VS/PR
8	b	BAL	54		EP/TM	101		RW	143	t	AS
9		AKG/EL	55		RW	102		VS/PR	143	b	EP
10		TDF	56	l & r	NHIL/R	103		SP/GC	144	t	VS/PR
11		AS/DL	58	t	TDF	104		NHIL/R	144	b	EP
12		TDF	59		TL	107		SB/AI	145		VS/PR
13		RW	60		RW/DT	108		TDF	146	t	TDF
14	t	AS/AN	61		NHIL/R	111		NHIL/R	146–147		INPRA/J-PL
14–15		TDF	62		TDF	113		SB/AI	148		GS
16	t	SP	63		RW	115		TL	149		SP
16	b	INPRA	64–65		NHIL/R	116		GS	150		VS/PR
17		NHIL/R	66		NHIL/R	117		TL	151		AS/KR
19		TDF	67		NHIL/R	119		TL/TP	152		TL/TP
20		TDF	68		TDF	120	t	AS/GP	153		VS/PR
21	t	NHIL/R	69		NHIL/R	120–121		SB/AI	154		GS/MG
21	b	TDF	70	l	NHIL/JM	122	t & b	SB/AI	155		MS
22		TDF	70	ct	AS/CC	123		INPRA	156	row1 l	SB/AI
24–25		NHIL/R	70	cb	TDF	124		EP/SP		row1 c	INPRA/SB
26	t & b	NHIL/R	70	r	RW	125		RW		row1 r	TDF
27		SB/AI	72–77		NHIL/R	126		SB/AI		row2 l	TL/TP
29		NHIL/R	78		SP	128		TDF		row2 r	RW
30		TDF	80		TL	129		SB/AI		row3 l	INPRA/NT
34		RW	81		TDF	130–131		NHIL/R		row3 r	RW
35		NHIL/R	82	t	NHIL/R	131		TL/TP		row4 l	TL/TP
36		RW	82	b	TDF	132		SB/AI		row4 c	TL/TP
38–39		NHIL/R	83		RW	133		TDF		row4 r	TL/TT
40–41		NHIL/R	84–85		NHIL/R	134		TDF	160		TDF
42–43		NHIL/R	86–87	b	NHIL/R	135		TL/TP			
44	t & b	TDF	87	t	SB/AI	136	t	AKG/AM			